The Disciplines of the Christian Life

✷ Eric Liddell ✷

The Disciplines of the
Christian Life

TRI∧NGLE

First published in the USA
by Abingdon Press 1985

First British edition 1985
Third impression 1987
Triangle/SPCK
Holy Trinity Church
Marylebone Road
London NW1 4DU

ACKNOWLEDGEMENT

Unless otherwise indicated, Scripture quotations are
from the Authorized Version, crown copyright.

British Library Cataloguing in Publication Data

Liddell, Eric
    The disciplines of the Christian life.
    1. Christian life
    I. Title
    248'.5   BV4509.5
    ISBN 0-281-04195-4

Typeset by Pioneer, East Sussex
Printed in Great Britain by
Hazell Watson & Viney Limited,
Member of the BPCC Group,
Aylesbury, Bucks

CONTENTS

A WORD ABOUT THIS BOOK

Herbert S. Long

According to Aristotle, character is shown only by free choice: in other words, while a person is under constraint, we learn nothing significant about his personal character. If this is so, then a remarkable revelation of character occurred when Eric Liddell gave up a distinguished athletic career at its high point and became a missionary to China. His decision became visible to the world after the Olympic Games of 1924, but it was no doubt in the making for years prior to that, as one can learn from the biographies by D. P. Thomson (1971), Sally Magnusson (1981), and Russell Ramsey (to be published).*

The award-winning film *Chariots of Fire* showed us, in a slightly fictionalized version, the problems and successes of two Olympic victors up to the time of their greatest achievement, without intending to portray their entire lives. Consequently, Eric Liddell's career as a missionary was only referred to; but that must have been for him the most significant part of his life, for which he gave up athletic fame. Seeing the movie made me wish to learn more about his subsequent years in China.

First I read the biographies. From them I learned that Mr Liddell had written three religious works: two pamphlets that were published in China in 1937 and 1942, and *A Manual of Christian Discipleship* that apparently had never been published. I determined to try to obtain copies of the pamphlets and, if possible, a photocopy of the unpublished work. The search required almost a year and developed a

*D. P. Thompson, *Eric H. Liddell: Athlete and Missionary* (Crieff, Scotland: The Research Unit, 1971); Sally Magnusson, *The Flying Scotsman* (London: Quartet Books, 1981); Russell Ramsey, *God's Joyful Runner*.

challenging aspect. It gradually became obvious that hardly any copies of the pamphlets ever left China, which is not surprising in view of the turmoil there in 1937 and in the whole world in 1942. Since no large library in the United States, Canada, or Great Britain possessed any of these documents, I tried the Council for World Mission in London (successor to the London Missionary Society, under which Mr Liddell served 1925—45), all the educational institutions in Great Britain which his biographies stated that he had attended, the Institute of Missionary Studies of Aberdeen University, and several of his friends to whom these institutions obligingly referred me, all without success. I began to wonder if his religious writings had disappeared without leaving a trace. Finally one of his friends put me in touch with his widow, Mrs Florence Liddell Hall, who kindly sent me copies of her copies of the two published pamphlets. The originals, which are in a private collection in California, are the only set that I know to exist in a determinate location. These brief pamphlets have now been entered in the computerized union library catalogue for the United States, and photocopies are in Freiberger Library of Case Western Reserve University, Cleveland, Ohio.

The third work, *A Manual of Christian Discipleship,* was the most highly regarded by Eric Liddell's friends. It circulated in manuscript in the internment camp where he died of a brain tumour on February 21, 1945; and, fortunately, manuscript copies of it still exist, from which it is now published for the first time. Thus, forty years after his premature death, Eric Liddell again speaks both to those who knew him personally and to the far larger number of us who did not.

HERBERT S. LONG
Professor of Classics
Case Western Reserve University

I REMEMBER ERIC LIDDELL

David J. Michell

If you saw the Academy Award-winning film *Chariots of Fire,* you will recall the jolt you felt as you read at the close these words about one of the heroes of the film:

> Eric Liddell, missionary,
> died in occupied China
> at the end of World War II.
> All of Scotland mourned.

I remember seeing Eric Liddell just the day before he died. For more than two years of our wartime captivity our school was interned in the same camp he was.* That day he was walking slowly under the trees near the camp hospital beside the open space where he had taught us children to play basketball and rounders. As usual, he had a smile for everyone, especially for us.

The athlete who had refused to run on a Sunday in the 1924 Olympic Games in Paris, but who later won the gold medal and created a world record in the 400 metres, was now — twenty-one years later at the age of forty-three — reaching the tape in his final race on earth. We knew nothing of the pain he was hiding, and he knew nothing of the brain tumour that was to take his life the next evening, February 21, 1945.

Eric Liddell's twenty years in China were eventful, to say the least. Within a year of his Olympic success, Eric had been farewelled from Edinburgh. More than a thousand people were unable to get in to the service. Deliberately

---

*The camp was Weihsien, Shantung, China. Our school was the Chefoo School for Missionary Children run by the China Inland Mission (now Overseas Missionary Fellowship).

walking away from the fame and glory that could have been his in Britain, he responded to God's call and went to China as a missionary with the London Missionary Society, following in his father's footsteps. For a number of years he taught science at the Anglo-Chinese College in Tientsin and then decided to tackle the more arduous task of rural evangelism, travelling many miles in rugged conditions by foot and bicycle.

On one occasion, as the hostilities between the Japanese and Chinese intensified in the late thirties, Eric Liddell heard about a wounded man who was dying in a derelict temple and whom none of the local people dared help for fear of reprisals from the Japanese. Despite natural fear of the consequences should they be caught, Eric persuaded a workman to accompany him with his cart to rescue the wounded man.

That night in a tumble-down Chinese inn, as the two men rested on their journey, God encouraged Eric through Luke 16.10: 'He that is faithful in that which is least is faithful also in much.'

When they reached the wounded man the next day, they lifted him on to the cart and began retracing their steps. Then, as they carefully led the swaying, creaking cart along the rough track, miraculously protected from encircling troops, they heard of another seriously injured man.

The second man had been one of six who were suspected of underground resistance and who had been lined up for beheading. Five knelt and were decapitated with the swift swish of the soldiers' swords. Because the sixth man refused to kneel, the sword missed its mark, inflicting, however, a deep gash from the back of the man's head to his mouth. He fell headlong and was left for dead. Villagers later came and helped him to a nearby shack. Though moving closer to danger, Eric and his companion reached the dying man, placed him in the shafts of the cart, and walked both desperately wounded men eighteen miles further to the mission hospital. Not only did this second man live, but he became a follower of Jesus Christ.

As conditions in China deteriorated in the weeks before the bombing of Pearl Harbour, Eric Liddell arranged for his wife and two children to leave China, planning himself to follow some months later. Safely in Canada, Florence Liddell gave birth to their third daughter, whom Eric never saw. Before he could get away, the Japanese armies had rounded up all 'enemy nationals' for internment in Weihsien, in the province of Shantung (Shandong), North China.

Sent to this same camp in Weihsien in August 1943 with many other missionaries' children, I will forever share with all the other hero-worshippers of my age that vivid memory of the man whom other prisoners described excitedly as the Olympic gold medalist who wouldn't run on a Sunday.

Eric Liddell stood out among the 1800 people packed into our camp, which measured only 150 by 200 yards. He was in charge of the building where we younger children, who had already been away from our parents for four years because of the war, lived with our teachers. He lived in the very crowded men's dormitory near us (each man had a space of only three by six feet) and supervised our daily roll-call when the guards came to count us. One day a week 'Uncle Eric' would look after us, giving our teachers (all missionaries of the China Inland Mission and all women) a break. His gentle face and warm smile, even as he taught us games with the limited equipment available, showed us how much he loved children and how much he missed his own.

Eric Liddell helped organize athletic meets. Despite the weakening physical conditions of the people as the war dragged on, the spirit of competition and camaraderie in sports was very good for us. Young and old watched excitedly, basking in the aura of Olympic glory as Eric Liddell ran in the race for veterans, his head thrown back in

11

his characteristic style, sailing through to victory.

Besides basketball, soccer and rounders, Eric Liddell taught us his favourite hymn:

> Be still, my soul: the Lord is on thy side;
> Bear patiently the cross of grief or pain;
> Leave to thy God to order and provide;
> In every change he faithful will remain.
> Be still, my soul: thy best, thy heavenly friend
> Through thorny ways leads to a joyful end.
>
> Katharina von Schlegel,
> trans. Jane L. Borthwick

These words were a great comfort to one of our missionaries who was not only separated from her husband throughout the war, but whose son was accidentally electrocuted by a bare wire running to one of the searchlight towers.

Eric Liddell often spoke to us on I Corinthians 13 and Matthew 5. These passages from the New Testament clearly portray the secret of his selfless and humble life. Only on rare occasions when requested would he speak of his refusal to run on Sunday and his Olympic record.

But once 'Uncle Eric' thrilled us with the story of the time he was persuaded to run in an extra race at an athletic meet in North China. The problem was that the race was scheduled just half an hour before his boat was due to leave to take him back to the college where he taught. He failed to have the boat's departure delayed but arranged for a taxi to take him from the track to the boat. Having won the race, Eric was just about to leap into the waiting taxi when the national anthem was played, followed straight off by the *Marseillaise,* forcing him to keep standing at attention as the minutes ticked by. The moment the music stopped he leaped into the taxi, and the vehicle sped off, reaching the wharf in under twenty minutes. By this time the boat was already moving out from the dock. But when a wave

12

momentarily lifted the boat nearer, Eric threw his bags on board and then took a mighty gazelle-like leap, managing to land on the back of the moving boat!

Not only did Eric Liddell organize sports and recreation, but throughout his time in the internment camp he helped many people by teaching and tutoring. He gave special care to the older people, the weak, and the ill, for whom the conditions in camp were especially trying. He was always involved in the Christian meetings which were a part of camp life. Despite the squalor of the open cesspools, rats, flies, and disease in the crowded camp, life took on a normal routine, though without the faithful and cheerful support of Eric Liddell, many people would never have been able to manage. Particularly grateful for his visits and encouragement were the daughter of a widow and a Roman Catholic nun, both critically ill and quarantined in the camp morgue.

Eric was one of those responsible for keeping law and order in camp. Ours was a world in microcosm, with prisoners representing nearly twenty nationalities. When we boys were caught climbing the tall trees in the Japanese part of the compound, how glad we were that it was he and our teachers who dealt with us, and not the Japanese guards!

As the months of captivity turned into years, there were many reasons why discouragement came over the camp. But, like the rest of us, Eric was buoyed by news from the outside that made its way inside, and he faithfully passed it on to us. We were all mystified as to how the news came — even our informant didn't know. We found out after the war was over, but Eric Liddell didn't live to hear the story. And what a story it was!

Some fourteen months before the war ended, two men in the camp escaped with the help of a coolie who came in to empty the cesspools and who was in league with others on the outside. Manoeuvring past the electrified wire in black, tight-fitting Chinese clothes, and crawling through a Chinese cemetery in the pitch darkness, they fled, making their way to South China, living in caves amid terrible conditions. It took them months to get back to the region of the camp with a radio without being discovered.

From their hiding place they dispatched news into the camp, writing it in code on a tiny piece of silk, rolling it up tightly and encapsuling it in a bit of rubber film. The same coolie who had helped the men escape earlier would push the pellet up his nose and out of sight, let himself be searched at the gate, wait until he reached a certain place in the camp, then blow his nose in the old-fashioned Chinese manner, and out would come this little pellet. Once he and his guard were out of sight, a Catholic priest would retrieve the capsule and later that night decode the news to be circulated secretly in the camp. In this way the whole camp knew when Germany had surrendered and also when the war with Japan was finally over.

But for Eric Liddell death came just months before liberation. He was buried in the little cemetery in the Japanese part of the camp where others who had died during internment had been laid to rest. I remember being part of the honour guard made up of children from the Chefoo and Weihsien schools. None of us will ever forget this man who was totally committed to putting God first, a man whose humble life combined muscular Christianity with radiant godliness.

What was his secret? He unreservedly committed his life to Jesus Christ as his Saviour and Lord. That friendship meant everything to him. By the flickering light of a peanut-oil lamp, early each morning he and a room-mate in the men's cramped dormitory studied the Bible and talked with God for an hour.

As a Christian, Eric Liddell's desire was to know God more deeply, and as a missionary, to make him known more fully.

DAVID J. MICHELL
Director for Canada
Overseas Missionary Fellowship

PUBLISHER'S NOTE

Eric Liddell's *The Disciplines of the Christian Life* was first published in the United States of America by Abingdon Press of Nashville, Tennessee, who were responsible for the necessary editing and research involved in preparing for publication a manuscript written more than forty years ago, and whose author is no longer living. For this British edition, we have restored certain minor stylistic and other changes made with an American public in mind, but otherwise have followed the Abingdon Press edition.

Triangle Books, SPCK

FROM THE EDITOR'S NOTE TO
THE ABINGDON PRESS EDITION

The substance of the book is as Eric Liddell wrote it. Some opening sentences and paragraphs have been added, as well as some bridges between sections.

The plan of the book as it came to us in manuscript has, for the most part, been followed. In 'The Year of Discipleship' section (the title is an editorial addition) each month or chapter begins with a general overview of the subject for the month, including an introduction to the scriptural teaching to be covered in the daily readings from the Bible. After the listing of the Scripture readings, some practical application of the teaching to daily living is discussed in more detail, some further helpful information is given, or one aspect of the subject is focused on more specifically.

Every effort has been made to check Eric Liddell's sources. The Reverend Alasdair J. Morton of the Church of Scotland Department of Education was very helpful in this regard. I also wish to thank Dr. Herbert S. Long for bringing the manuscript to Abingdon's attention, Mr. David Michell for his interest and help and for providing his personal memories of Eric Liddell, and Mrs. Florence Liddell Hall, Eric Liddell's widow, who provided us with the manuscript. Unfortunately, Mrs. Hall died before the book went to press.

Eric Liddell

The Disciplines of the Christian Life

PREFACE

In this book I am attempting to do three things:

- To place before people the limited amount of Christian knowledge that every Christian should have;

- To help people apply their knowledge to daily life; to live according to the light they have;

- To develop the devotional life so as to create basic Christian thinking on subjects of conduct, action, outlook, and attitudes.

The Christian life should be a life of growth. I believe the secret of growth is to develop the devotional life.

This involves setting aside each day a time for prayer and Bible study. The time need not be long, but it should be unhurried. We should come to it in an honest spirit, prepared to face the challenge of God's Word as it lays down a way of life, and prepared to face any inconsistencies in our lives which make them un-Christlike.

The material in each chapter is not meant to be read over once only. It should be read or pondered over many times. (If you use the suggested Scriptures listed in each chapter for your daily reading, then you might want to reread the introductory section daily. The twelve chapters and the Scripture passages will take you through a year.) In future days, the subject will be part of your automatic (unconscious) thinking — creating an awakened, enlightened conscience. Anything done contrary to its spirit will immediately pull you up as being inconsistent with our basic thought. This careful attention and repetition is the method used in learning any new subject. It is the method used in becoming proficient in any game. As Isaiah says:

Precept upon precept, precept upon precept;
   line upon line, line upon line;
      here a little, and there a little; (Isaiah 28.13)

How much more should this be so for the greatest of all ventures, the art of living a Christian life.

After reading the Scripture passages, *ponder over them, taking special note of their application to present day circumstances and the problems associated with your daily life as a Christian.*

I have tried to give the source of all the quotations. I feel I am indebted to so many influences, books and people that it is impossible to mention them all by name.

ERIC H. LIDDELL

PART 1

The Life of Discipleship

God is love. (1 John 4.8)

By this shall all men know that ye are my disciples, if ye have love one to another.   (John 13.35)

Love is very patient, very kind.
Love knows neither envy nor jealousy.
Love is not forward or self-assertive.
Love is not boastful or conceited, gives itself no airs.
Love is never rude, never selfish, never irritated.
Love never broods over wrongs.
Love thinketh no evil.
Love is never glad when others go wrong.
Love finds no pleasure in injustice but rejoices in the truth.
Love is always slow to expose; it knows how to be silent.
Love is always eager to believe the best about a person.
Love is full of hope, full of patient endurance.
Love never fails.
(1 Corinthians 13, paraphrase)

Love is of God; and every one that loveth is born of God, and knoweth God. He that loveth not knoweth not God; for God is love.   (1 John 4.7-8)

God is love; and he that dwelleth in love dwelleth in God, and God in him.   (1 John 4.16)

If a man say, I love God, and hateth his brother, he is a liar; for he that loveth not his brother whom he hath seen, how can he love God whom he hath not seen?   (1 John 4.20)

Whoso hath this world's good, and seeth his brother have need, and shutteth up his bowels of compassion from him, how dwelleth the love of God in him? My little children, let us not love in word, neither tongue; but in deed and in truth.   (1 John 3.17-18)

Thou shalt love the Lord thy God with all thy heart, and with all thy soul, and with all thy strength, and with all thy mind; and thy neighbour as thyself.   (Luke 10.27)

WHAT IS DISCIPLESHIP?

The Key to Knowing God

A disciple is one who knows God personally, and who learns from Jesus Christ, who most perfectly revealed God. One word stands out from all others as the key to knowing God, to having his peace and assurance in your heart; it is *obedience*.

Obedience to God's will is the secret of spiritual knowledge and insight. It is not willingness to know, but willingness to *do* (obey) God's will that brings enlightenment and certainty regarding spiritual truth. 'If any man will do [obey] his will, he shall know of the doctrine, whether it be of God, or whether I speak of myself' (John 7.17).

Here are some questions to ask yourself. If I know something to be true, am I prepared to follow it even though it is contrary to what I want, to what I have previously said or held to be true? Will I follow it even if it means loss of face, owning that I was wrong? Will I follow if it means being laughed at by friend or foe, if it means personal financial loss or some kind of hardship?

Following truth leads to God, for truth is of God.

Obedience is the secret of being conscious that God guides you personally, If in the quiet of your heart you feel something should be done, stop and consider whether it is in line with the character and teaching of Jesus. If so, obey that impulse to do it, and in doing so you will find it was God guiding you.

Every Christian should live a God-guided life. If you are not guided by God, you will be guided by someone or something else. The Christian who hasn't the sense of guidance in his life is missing something vital.

To obey God's will was like food to Jesus, refreshing his

mind, body, and spirit. 'My meat is to do the will of him that sent me' (John 4.34). We can all have the same experience if we make God's will the dominant purpose in our lives.

Take obedience with you into your time of prayer and meditation, *for you will know as much of God, and only as much of God, as you are willing to put into practice*. There is a great deal of truth in the hymn 'Trust and obey'.

> When we walk with the Lord
> In the light of His Word
> What a glory He sheds on our way!
> While we *do his good will*,
> He abides with us still,
> *And with all who will trust and obey.*

J. H. Sammis (italics added)

Applying the Moral Tests

Search me, O God, and know my heart: try me, and know my thoughts. (Psalm 139.23)

Examine yourselves, whether ye be in the faith. (2 Corinthians 13.5)

God speaks to people through the moral law. If we break these laws and excuse ourselves for doing so, the presence and guidance of God lose their reality in our lives: the freedom and radiance of the Christian life depart.

Here are four tests of the moral law by which to measure ourselves—and so obey the biblical commands.

Am I truthful? Are there any conditions under which I will or do tell a lie? Can I be depended on to tell the truth no matter what the cost? Yes or no? Don't hedge, excuse, explain. Yes or no?

Am I honest? Can I be absolutely trusted in money matters? In my work even when no one is looking? With other people's reputations? Yes or no? With myself, or do I rationalize and become self-defensive?

Am I pure? In my habits? In my thought life? In my motives? In my relations with the opposite sex? Yes or no?

Am I selfish? In the demands I make on my family, wife, husband, or associates? Am I badly balanced; full of moods, cold today and warm tomorrow?

Do I indulge in nerves that spoil both my happiness and the happiness of those around me?

Am I unrestrained in my pleasures, the kind I enjoy without considering the effect they have on my soul?

Am I unrestrained in my work, refusing to take reasonable rest and exercise?

Am I unrestrained in small self-indulgences, letting myself become the slave of habits, however harmless they may appear to me?

What am I living for—self, money, place, power? Or are my powers at the disposal of human need, dedicated to the Kingdom of God on earth?

Let us put ourselves before ourselves and look at ourselves. *The bravest moment of a man's life is the moment when he looks at himself objectively without wincing, without complaining.*

Self-examination which does not result in action is dangerous. *What am I going to do about what I see?* The action called for is surrender—of ourselves to God.

Surrender

What Do I Surrender?

The Initial Surrender

1. *The Negatives.* I become convinced that up to the present, with myself in control of my life I haven't got

anywhere. I see that the life that is joyous, rich, and has a worthwhile goal is the life with Jesus in control. God asks me to surrender my control.

I become convinced that my life is not really controlled by myself but by sin. Its power dominates my life. I do what I afterwards loathe. God asks me to surrender myself to him.

I become conscious that the dominant factor in my life, the factor on which I make decisions, is not God but something or someone else. It might, for instance, be laziness. God asks the surrender of that first place to him so that in future I will base my actions and reactions on what he desires.

Habits, outlooks, attitudes, moods, self-indulgences of one kind or another, which I know are not the best, nor in line with the life and teaching of Jesus, are constantly cropping up and causing inhibitions or conflicts in my life. God asks the surrender of these.

2. *Completeness*. The more complete that first surrender is, the greater the chance of quick and continuous growth in the Christian life.

3. *Surrender is not the new birth*. The new birth should be simultaneous with, or closely following, the act of surrender, but is not identical with it. The new birth is the great work God does in us in renewing our natures. Surrender is our part.

Subsequent Surrenders

Although at the time we may feel that the first surrender was complete, we begin to realize there is *much more we never dreamed of* that needs surrendering. New situations arise; new problems face us; new sacrifices are asked, and we find they are not faced without a struggle. For a time we may hardly be aware of them. Slowly the conscience detects the leading of God. We do not fully face it because it is inconvenient or uncomfortable to do so. God leads on till we know it means either surrender and going forward in the Christian life or avoiding it and finding his guidance less distinct and our Christian lives less victorious.

Daily Surrender

It is helpful to start each new day with a question like the following clearly before you: 'Have I surrendered this new day to God, and will I seek and obey the guidance of the Holy Spirit throughout its hours?' Wait until, with the full consent of your will, you can say, 'I have; I will.'

How Do I Surrender?

It is when we come to the question of how to surrender that we meet with difficulties. It would be best for you to discuss this with your minister or some friend you know who is living the kind of Christian life you admire. Here are some suggestions to help you.

1. The ideal way would be to take what you feel should be surrendered and in prayer, on your knees before God, tell him all. Hide nothing; be honest in your attitude towards it and towards God. Wait on your knees till you know you have God's forgiveness and that your surrender has been accepted.

Although this is the ideal way, it is often the most difficult. It is difficult to be honest with yourself, to be sure that you really want, with all your heart, to forsake the particular thing on your mind and conscience. *Besides, that might just be a symptom sin and not the root sin*, in which case it often means surrender and fall.

2. Many of us have found the surrender more satisfactory and complete by first sharing it, that is, talking it over with a friend who understands. This is hard. I know it is hard. It

31

strikes at one of the deep-rooted sins, namely pride, and that is what makes it so difficult. It seems harder to tell someone else than to tell God. Yet it shouldn't be. We often take things to God in such a way that it costs us very little, more in the attitude of justifying our failure than confessing our guilt. It is here that a true friend can be so helpful, bringing out the points that need to be surrendered. Together turn in prayer to make your surrender to God. In quiet, wait for God, to know what you should do about it.

3. When surrender is being made, whether alone or with another person, the mind should not be focused only on our act, but also on God's forgiveness. *The Cross, and what has been done for us by God, is far greater than anything we are doing.* We are saved by grace and by grace alone.

Surrender means the end of the great rebellion of our wills. We capitulate; God can act.

4. *Do not try to limit God* to the smallness of your prejudices. God honours many ways of surrendering. Do not try to avoid one method because it hurts your pride. Pride must go. You may find you have to come back to the very method you have been trying to avoid.

> For the love of God is broader
>   Than the measures of man's mind;
> And the heart of the Eternal
>   Is most wonderfully kind.
>
> But we make his love too narrow
>   By false limits of our own;
> And we magnify his strictness
>   With a zeal he will not own.
>
> There is plentiful redemption
>   In the blood that has been shed;
> There is joy for all the members
>   In the sorrows of the Head.   F. W. Faber

Characteristics of a Disciple

Righteousness and love are the two central pillars of religion. They are the two attributes of God that are inseparable. They are the two characteristics that God longs to see harmoniously united in every individual. A third indispensable characteristic of a disciple is humility.

Righteousness

Righteousness includes honesty. It always tells the truth. It prefers to tell the truth and suffer than lie and escape the punishment. If telling the truth brings another into trouble, it usually prefers to be silent and suffer.

It is honest with money. Small as well as large amounts are safe in its hands. It is especially careful with other people's or public money.

It is honest with other people's things. Articles borrowed are returned; money loaned is repaid.

It is honest in business. Full weight is given in selling; goods are not adulterated; the truth about the articles is told.

It is honest in speech. Its 'yes' means 'yes', its 'no' means 'no'. It is honest in work; it works as well whether it is on its own or supervised.

Righteousness includes sincerity. Not only is the action honest, but the motive that lies behind it is sincere. There is no duplicity. It stands by its word. Its word is its bond.

Righteousness includes justice. It is always just in its dealings with others. The rich and poor, the strong and weak, the powerful and powerless are all treated alike. It never takes advantage of its position but judges according to right and wrong. It never accepts bribes. It never lends money at high interest; it seeks a just price.

Righteousness seeks to be right with God. It reverences

33

God but has no need to fear him, for it is willing to bring all its actions and motives into the light of God's presence. It seeks first of all to please not man but God.

Righteousness seeks to be right with man. It desires to put aside everything that causes barriers between man and man. (This is not always possible, but we can do all that can be done on our side towards this end.) Side, snobbishness, rudeness, dislikes, revenge and attitudes which can be put right he seeks, with all his heart, to put right.

Righteousness seeks to put aside all known sin, failings, weaknesses. It desires, with the whole heart, to put aside all that might hinder its growth in the Christian life; all that limits its usefulness—laziness, anger; all that blurs its vision —pride, jealousy, envy, carelessness of other people's needs, selfishness; all that weakens its will—habits known to be wrong, decisions made through fear, etc. Do I want righteousness of this kind?

> Blessed are they which do hunger and thirst after righteousness: for they shall be filled. (Matthew 5.6)

Love

> By this shall all men know that ye are my disciples, if ye have love one to another. (John 13.35)

Love is patient to all. It suffers all the weakness, ignorance, errors and pettiness of the children of God. It suffers all the malice and wickedness of the world, and that not just for a short time but to the end.

Love is kind. It is always ready to go out of its way to help. It longs to reduce people's burdens by willingly and joyfully sharing their sorrows and hardships. It throws out a great offensive of love to break down the barriers that separate man from man.

Love does not think more highly of itself than it should. It

34

recognizes that every gift and talent comes from God. It has nothing to boast of but the goodness of God. Love recognizes the responsibility to use and develop these gifts but not to become proud, arrogant, patronizing or to give itself airs because of them.

Love is never rude. It is never willingly offensive. It is polite and courteous.

Love is never irritated. Outward provocations will constantly occur, but love does not yield to these; it triumphs over them. In all trials it looks to Jesus and is more than conqueror in his strength. (See the times when Jesus was angry and learn the difference between anger and righteous indignation.)

Love is never selfish—never selfish for praise, popularity, or pity; never selfish in the desire for, or use of, money and possessions; never self-centred in thought life, in planning just for itself, its comfort, its convenience; never self-opinionated, seeking to impose its point of view, its way or its plan on others.

Love never broods over wrongs. It does not ponder over them so as to magnify them and increase the feeling for revenge. No, it takes them to God in prayer; it surrenders them to him and has the attitude of forgiveness to the person concerned.

Love thinks no evil. It casts out all evil surmisings, all readiness to believe evil. It is frank, open, unsuspicious; and, as it cannot design, so neither does it fear evil.

Love is never glad when others go wrong. Apply this to the man with whom you are competing, your opponent, your enemy. Never be glad when others make a wrong move, an unwise step contrary to God's law of righteousness and love which leads to their downfall.

Love rejoices in the truth. It seeks and rejoices in the truth even if it means owning oneself to be in the wrong.

Love is always slow to expose; it knows when to be silent.

The merciful man does not willingly mention or expose the faults or failings of others. He hates and keeps away from all gossip, backbiting and evil-speaking. Before passing on evil of others he first asks, *Is it true? Is it loving? Is it necessary?* and only repeats it if he feels it is absolutely necessary that it should be mentioned.

Love is always eager to believe the best, to put the best construction on everything. Even when the action, motive, and intention are all shown to be evil, love still hopes that the person will repent and come back to bask in God's loving forgiveness.

Love never fails — never, for God is love.

Humility

Humility is a distinctive Christian virtue. It is an indispensable virtue in the New Testament, where it is closely connected with the teaching and example of Jesus.

Humility has no self-conscious pride about it. It does not shut its eyes to its faults and limitations. It is prepared to recognize and confess how it has fallen short of God's plan, or disobeyed God's law or its own conscience. It sees itself in the light of a holy God. It does not compare its life with other people's lives.

Humility is not afraid to learn new lessons and make new beginnings. It has no mock-humility about it saying, 'I can't do this . . .' when all the time it wants to be pressed more to do so. Nor does it say, 'I can't do . . .' because it is afraid of loss of face if it fails, or because people will laugh.

Humility is not out to justify its actions; it does not have a defensive attitude to life. 'He [the lawyer], willing to justify himself, said . . .' (Luke 10.29).

Humility looks at its sins (self-examination) but also *looks beyond them* to the Saviour from sin and casts itself upon his mercy. Sometimes people are too proud to cast themselves on God's mercy. Pride is the great enemy of humility.

Humility looks at its merits, gifts, and talents but also *looks beyond them to God*, the Author of every good and perfect gift, and renders all the glory to God (see Matthew 5.16).

Humility is powerful, for it is based on the sense of being absolutely dependent on the grace of God. That is why a good Christian has such a serene and confident spirit, combined with the utmost humility. He aims very high, attempts great things and yet without proud looks or thoughts, because he is not thinking of himself, but of God. 'I can do all things through Christ which strengthen me' (Philippians 4.13). He has the simple, childlike heart, because he depends so much on his heavenly Father.

Humility is not worried about 'face'. It is prepared to own a fault, a mistake, make an apology, or make restitution if it has wronged anyone.

[Thoughts based on *Christian Faith and Practice* by A. C. Craig, O. B. Milligan, D. M. Baillie.]

My Creed

I believe in God the Father, Almighty, Creator, infinitely holy and loving, who has a plan for the world, a plan for my life, and some daily work for me to do.

I believe in Jesus, the Christ, the Son of God, as Example, Lord, and Saviour.

I believe in the Holy Spirit who is able to guide my life so that I may know God's will; and I am prepared to allow him to guide and control my life.

I believe in God's law that I should love the Lord my God with *all* my heart, and with *all* my soul, and with *all* my mind, and with *all* my strength; and my neighbour as myself.

I believe it is God's will that the whole world should be without any barriers of race, colour, class, or anything else that breaks the spirit of fellowship.

To believe means to believe with the mind and heart, to accept, and to act accordingly on that basis.

Aids to Your Daily Quiet Time

One way to know God is to spend time with him each day. Set aside a specific time for prayer and Bible study, and plan to stick to it every day. A morning quiet time will help to set the course for the day. Ask yourself, 'Have I surrendered this new day to God, and will I seek and obey the guidance of the Holy Spirit throughout its hours?' Wait till you can honestly say, 'Yes, I have surrendered the day to God. I will follow where he guides, and I will do his will as he reveals it to me. Father, help me this day to fulfill this vow.'

Here are some suggestions to help you make the most of that time.

1. *Be still.* God, the source of all truth and love, is here. Take time to realize his presence. Be glad that *he speaks when we listen*, and *hears when we pray*. Thank him for his Spirit living in us. 'Our Father, which art in heaven, Hallowed be thy name.'

2. *For what are you especially thankful this morning?* Name some of God's gifts to you: friends, family, lessons learned, challenge of difficulties, new responsibilities, etc. Thank him particularly for Christ, and the new freedom he has given you. 'Love the Lord your God with your whole heart, soul, mind, and strength.'

3. *Accept Christ into your life for today*, with all his qualities of outgoing love, honesty, purity, and unselfishness, and with his passion to do God's will. Where you failed yesterday to measure up to Christ's standards, be honest about it; accept promptly God's forgiveness and release in Christ; *get up and go on* in his strength. 'Create in me a clean heart, O God' (Psalm 51.10). 'Go, and sin no more' (John 8.11).

4. In the light of God's love and the world's needs, *what new responsibilities* for people and situations does God want you to take today? *Find out his plan*. Make notes of things he wants you to do, people to pray for, etc. *Listen to God and obey fearlessly* throughout the day. 'In the world you have trouble, but courage!—I have conquered the world' (John 16.33, Moffatt).

5. *What new message has God for you from the Bible this morning?* What new light does your study throw on his plan for the world, and your part in it? 'If anyone loves me, he will obey my word' (John 14.15, Weymouth).

6. *Remember your duty today is to witness for God*, by example, character, in the home, at your work, and in your spare time. Be ready also to witness to God's grace, mercy, and guidance. Be alert to pass on any message that would help or cheer another. You have prayed, 'Thy kingdom come'. How are you going to help God answer that prayer?

As a further aid to Christian living, I would urge everyone to learn the following Scripture passages by heart:

Exodus 20.1-17	The Commandments
Matthew 5.1-12	The Beatitudes
Matthew 6.9-13	The Lord's Prayer
1 Corinthians 13.1-13	Paul's great passage on love
Psalm 23.1-6	'The Lord is my shepherd'

Everyone should learn the names and order of the books of the Old and New Testaments so as to be able to turn to them quickly.

❇ PART 2 ❇

A Year of Discipleship

GOD

The Nature of God

God is a Spirit

No man can see God with his eyes. No distance can separate anyone from God. I can hide nothing from him. He knows me, even the hidden secrets of my heart. 'Let the words of my mouth, and the meditation of my heart, be acceptable in thy sight, O Lord' (Psalm 19.14).

God is the Creator

'The earth is the Lord's, and the fulness thereof; the world, and they that dwell therein' (Psalm 24.1). God was, and is, and shall ever be behind everything. Beauty, order, fertility, life are all his work. He is the great Creator. He is the heavenly Giver. He is a God of order and of law and he works through his natural laws; that is one reason why we can come to know him.

God is Righteous

'God is light, and in him is no darkness at all' (1 John 1.5). God is a God with character. In him there can be nothing that is wrong or evil. He is just and pure, true and righteous, as are his laws. His holiness awes us.

God is Love

The whole nature of God is love. We can never separate this from any of his other attributes. Jesus taught us to

43

think of him as 'Our Father'—greater, wiser, better than any father we could imagine. In his love he guards and guides and educates us.

Man, the Image of God

God made us in his own image, that is, with the seeds of righteousness and love in our hearts which should grow and develop into a natural beauty of character. He has made us with a deep desire for fellowship with him, able to return love for love, and knowing that we ought to follow his law. He has made us restless till we find rest in him by trusting, depending upon, obeying, and loving him.

The Lost Image

Sin, and sin only, separates me from God. God has given man free will. Man may choose to disobey God's law, to slight God's love, to follow his own desires. All this is sin. Sin brings its own punishment just as surely as breaking any of the laws of nature brings punishment. Man loses the image of God. Sin separates man from God, and because of this, man fears to meet his Maker, trying to avoid him. Nothing hurts God more than this, for he is 'Our Father'. The Lover, God, has lost the one whom he loves. His love will stop short of nothing till the lost one is brought back again into the right relationship with the Father.

Lost Image Renewed

Men are reconciled to God. God's love is revealed in many ways, but, greatest of all, in the life and death of Jesus. Here is a righteous and loving God making the final appeal of righteousness and love to draw man back to himself so that he may renew his image within man. 'Be renewed in the spirit of your minds, and put on the new nature, created after the likeness of God in true righteousness and holiness' (Ephesians 4.23-24).

God's Moral Law

God's moral law forms the basis of all law. No nation or people can neglect it and hope to prosper. Some 3,500 years ago God, through Moses, gave this law to bind together a slave people who had just been set free, and through whom God hoped to reveal more clearly to the world what his will and purpose was. The law is summarized in what we call the Ten Commandments (Exodus 20; Deuteronomy 5).

God's Law Summarized

Thou shalt have no other gods before me.
Thou shalt not worship idols.
Thou shalt not take the Name of the Lord in vain.
Remember the Sabbath day to keep it holy.
Honour thy father and thy mother.
Thou shalt not kill.
Thou shalt not commit adultery.
Thou shalt not steal.
Thou shalt not bear false witness.
Thou shalt not covet what belongs to another.

The Positive Spirit of the Law

Wherewith shall I come before the Lord, and bow myself before the high God? . . . He hath showed thee, O man, what is good; and what doth the Lord require of thee, but to do justly, and to love mercy, and to walk humbly with thy God? (Micah 6.6, 8)

Do justly. See pages 33-4, 'Righteousness'.
Love mercy. See pages 34-6, 'Love'.
Walk humbly with thy God. See pages 36-7, 'Humility'.

The Law of the Spirit—The Law of Liberty

If ye be led of the Spirit, ye are not under the law. . . . But the fruit of the Spirit is love, joy, peace, longsuffering, gentleness, goodness, faith, meekness, temperance: against such there is no law. (Galatians 5.18, 22-23)

Communicating with God

We communicate with God through prayer and Bible study. The best way is to decide upon a definite time for your prayer time, preferably in the early morning, and keep it sacred. Build the habits of your life around that period. Do not allow it to be crowded out by other things. Those who, neglecting the fixed time for prayer, say they can pray at all times, will probably end in praying at no time. But if you keep the fixed period, it should influence the whole day.

1. *In the beginning of the prayer period, be silent.* Let your mind relax, allowing it to roam across your life to see whether it stops at anything wrong. If so, determine in God's strength that you will right it. Make sure you do right it. If nothing is shown to be wrong, you are ready for bold praying. See 1 John 3.21.

2. *Then bathe your thought in God's Word.* It will wash the dust from your eyes and give you insight. Thus you will get right attitudes and will pray right prayers. God will be bringing your thoughts into line with his thoughts, your purposes with his purposes.

3. *Take a pen or pencil and write down what comes to you.*

Pore over God's Word. That pen is a sign of your faith that something will come, and it will. Don't read hurriedly. Every word is precious. Pause, assimilate. When a person hurries through a wood, few birds and animals appear. They hide. But if he sits down and waits, they come out. It will be so with reading the Bible and praying. 'Prayer is a time exposure of the soul to God.' Expose your inmost being to his Word. Be willing to obey, and *obey*.

[Thoughts based on *Victorious Living* by E. Stanley Jones.]

4. *The outcome of the prayer time should be action.* You should have some definite, concrete work to do. Often the actions are small, but they demand some sacrifice of time, or test your patience and love. Do them. Keeping a record may prove helpful.

I would suggest the discipline of rising half an hour earlier than usual and giving the time to prayer, meditation, and Bible study. Be careful, however, not to fall into the habit of thinking God can only guide you at this one special time, or any one special time. Be careful, too, about your attitude to others who differ from you regarding the time they find most helpful. Be prepared to change the time of your prayer if the circumstances of your life lead you to feel it necessary or advisable.

Scripture Readings

The passages that I have listed below are not long ones. After you have read each day's reading, go back over the appropriate discussion in the chapter. Read the scriptures several times. Have a Bible you are not afraid to mark. Mark any passage that specially attracts your attention. Stop and ponder over it. Seek God, and God's Word for you, with your whole heart. Be alert and sensitive to his guidance. 'Ye shall seek me, and find me, *when ye shall search for me with all your heart*' (Jeremiah 29.13, italics added).

God's Moral Law

Day				
	1	Psalm 19.7-14	The value of the law	Psalm 119.1-16
	2	Exodus 20.1-3	One God	Luke 18.18-27
	3	Exodus 20.1-6	No idols	Acts 17.16-31
	4	Exodus 20.7	Swearing and blasphemy	Matthew 5.33-37
	5	Exodus 20.8-11	The sabbath	Matthew 12.9-13
	6	Exodus 20.12	Filial piety	Mark 7.1-13
	7	Exodus 20.13	Murder, anger, revenge	Matthew 5.21-26
	8	Exodus 20.14	Adultery	Matthew 5.27-32
	9	Exodus 20.15	Stealing	Acts 5.1-11
	10	Exodus 20.16	False witness	Matthew 26.57-68
	11	Exodus 20.17	Coveting, envy, jealousy	Luke 12.13-21

Prayer

Day			
	12	Matthew 6.5-8	Sincerity and truth are first essentials
	13	Matthew 6.9-15	The Lord's Prayer and forgiveness
	14	Matthew 18.21-35	Prayer and the forgiving spirit
	15	Matthew 18.19-20	Where true prayer is, Jesus is
	16	Matthew 17.14-21	The need of prayer
	17	Luke 18.1-8	Importunate prayer
	18	Luke 18.9-14	Humility and prayer
	19	Matthew 26.36-46	Prayer and God's will
	20	Philippians 4.4-9	No worry, share all with God
	21	James 5.13-18	The value of prayer

The Word of God, Bible Study

Day	22	Psalm 119.9-16	Power to keep me
	23	Psalm 119.41-48	Courage to witness
	24	Psalm 119.97-104	Wisdom and enjoyment
	25	Psalm 119.105-112	Light for the daily path
	26	Psalm 119.161-168	A rich treasure store
	27	Mark 7.1-13	The meaning hidden by our traditions
	28	Acts 8.26-39	Understandest thou?
	29	Luke 4.1-13	Use of the Bible in temptation
	30	2 Timothy 3.14-17; 1.5	The Bible in the home
	31	2 Peter 1.16-21	Inspiration

(Use pages 38-40, 'Aids to Your Daily Quiet Time' day by day: it should help your prayer time to become more vital.)

THE LIFE OF JESUS

Jesus' life is the most beautiful life there has ever been. Born in a stable, brought up in a humble home, working in a carpenter's shop, he forged the thoughts that were to *revolutionize the world.*

The Gospel records are mainly concerned with the last three years of Jesus' life, when he left the workshop to give God's message to the world. Those in authority refused his message; he was betrayed by one of his disciples and, when arrested, deserted by the others; brought before Pilate for trial; and brutally crucified between two thieves.

He preached the kingdom of heaven among men.

He healed as the natural outlet to his love.

He taught, largely by parables, giving to people the basic foundations of life and thought.

He loved, even to the end, praying as they crucified him, 'Father, forgive them; for they know not what they do'. (Luke 23.34).

He gathered around him twelve disciples and to these he gave his teaching by word, act and example, leading them, as a wise teacher, step by step to know him and his divine commission, and finally to realize their share in that commission.

Four of the twelve disciples—namely, Peter, Andrew, James and John—take a more prominent place in the Gospel stories. They seem to have been on more intimate terms with Jesus. About some of the Twelve we know very little, but it is generally accepted that none of them came from the rich and influential classes.

They failed him at his death, but with the resurrection

and Pentecost they awoke to the meaning of the message he had been trying to give them, and went out to conquer the world.

At least one good book on the life of Jesus should be read by everyone, Christian and non-Christian.

Philosophy! He gives to man a philosophy of life.

History! He stands as a great landmark in history.

Religion! He shows how a person can live a life of intimate, personal relationship with God.

Mark's Gospel—The Earliest Gospel

Mark's Gospel was the first to appear. There is a very ancient and reliable tradition which tells us that 'Mark became the interpreter of Peter' and that he 'wrote down accurately everything that he remembered' from Peter's discourses and sermons. That is of the utmost importance. It gives us a picture of young John Mark accompanying the great apostle on his preaching tours. We see Mark listening again and again to the story of the life and death of Jesus as it came from Peter's lips, until he knew that story by heart himself, and was living in the atmosphere of it; and when at last death claimed his great friend and leader, and Mark was left alone, he wrote the story down. It is a great thing to know that behind it stands the witness of Peter, one of the Master's most intimate friends.

After the death of Peter, which many believe took place at Rome in the persecution under Nero in AD 64, what is more natural than that the Christians in Rome would desire to perpetuate the teaching which Peter had given them? Natural, too, would be their wish to preserve in permanent and written form the life and teaching of Jesus Christ. For those were perilous times; there were opponents, both Jewish and heathen, to be refuted; and with the passing of years the number of eye-witnesses of the Lord was becoming smaller and smaller.

Mark's Gospel was written about AD 65. It was written at Rome and was mainly intended for Gentiles (not Jews) and especially Romans. Notice in regard to this:

- Latin forms not occurring in other Gospels;
- Jewish terms and customs explained;
- omission of all references to Jewish law.

The words, 'The Gospel According to St Mark', which stand in our Authorized Version at the beginning of this little book, are a later addition. Mark himself gave no name. The evangelists were not seeking literary reputation. Their passion for the glory of Christ had submerged every thought of self; they were not concerned that the world should know from whose hands the story had come. Earthly fame was nothing to these men: the beauty of Christ meant everything to them.

[Thoughts based on *The Life and Teaching of Jesus Christ* by James S. Stewart.]

Scripture Readings

As you read these passages about the life of Jesus, note the way he treated people; how he was busy but not hurried; how he faced life's problems but was not worried. His serenity showed that he was conscious of having sufficient power for every emergency. What was the secret? Am I like this? Why not? Can I become like this? Yes, his disciples did.

The Life of Jesus — The Gospel According to Mark
Day 1   Mark 1.1-8   John the Baptist
    2   Mark 1.9-15   Baptism, temptation and preaching

The Training of the Disciples

Are you using 'Aids to Your Daily Quiet Time', each day?

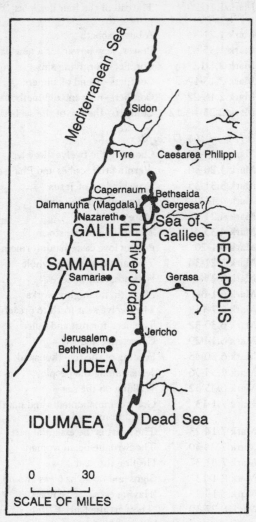

Palestine During the Time of Jesus

Do you find it helpful? If so, why not suggest this method to your friends? They might find it helpful too.

The Land of Palestine

As you read the story of Jesus, *whenever a place is mentioned look for it on the map.* In this way you will soon become familiar with Palestine, the country in which Jesus lived. It is a small country about 140 miles long and varying in width from 25 miles in the north to about 80 miles in the south.

Palestine has three main divisions. In the north is Galilee, where Jesus lived for the larger part of his life. In the south is Judea, with its capital, Jerusalem, where Jesus was finally put to death. Between these two lies Samaria. The Samaritans were not pure Jews. There was a deep-rooted enmity between the Jews and the Samaritans.

About seven hundred years before the birth of Jesus, Israel (the part now called Galilee and Samaria) was conquered by the Assyrians. Thousands of the people were carried away as captives, their places being taken by the Assyrian colonists. These colonists intermarried with the remaining Israelites, took on many of their customs, and gradually became one united people. They formed the race known as the Samaritans.

Because of this strong feeling of hatred, Jews travelling from Galilee to Judea would often prefer to avoid passing through Samaria by crossing the river Jordan, travelling down on its east side and recrossing the river when they were approaching Judea.

THE LIFE OF JESUS (continued)

The Cross

The Twelve now believe Jesus to be the Christ, the Messiah, the leader promised in Old Testament prophecy. But a deeper truth has yet to be learned— *Jesus is the Son of God. The stupendous mystery of the cross has now to be revealed.*

When faced by the Cross, men have asked, 'Why?' Our Lord says it 'must' be so. Only through the final challenge and suffering can he enter into glory and establish for ever God's kingdom in man, lifting us with him into glory.

On the rock of a solid faith Christ can now build. So he began to teach them the fact of his Cross. Can we imagine what a shock this was to Peter? He had confessed Jesus to be the Messiah, but the messiahship he visualized was one of power and splendour, not of a cross and death. In his revulsion of feeling he remonstrated with our Lord. But Jesus answered in effect: *'You think like man, not like God.'*

The Cross Must Be. No Cross. No Crown.

The meaning of the Cross never dawned on the disciples until after they had seen it enacted and the resurrection had taken place. Then it dawned slowly. A glory began to shine around this Cross, where men saw revealed the magnitude of God's love and the awfulness of their own sin. Nor was that all, for here was the Lamb of God taking away the sin of the world. *Forgiveness!* O blessed word to those bowed down by the guilt of sin. As Bunyan's Pilgrim says,

> Thus far did I come laden with my sin;
> Nor could aught ease the grief that I was in
> Till I came hither: What a place is this!
> Must here be the beginning of my bliss?
> Must here the burden fall from off my back?
> Must here the strings that bound it to me crack?
> Blest Cross! Blest Sepulchre! Blest rather be
> The Man that there was put to shame for me!

People use different terminology in speaking of the Cross—'the cross', 'the blood', 'the death', 'the sacrifice' of Christ, but these are really just different terms for the same thing.

Paul was very clear as to the place the Cross played in the world. All history led up to it; all history looks back to it.

The Cross Meets Man's Greatest Need

For the preaching of the cross is to them that perish foolishness; but unto us which are saved it is the power of God. (1 Corinthians 1.18)

For if, when we were enemies, we were reconciled to God by the death of his Son, much more, being reconciled, we shall be saved by his life. (Romans 5.10)

Who was delivered for our offences, and was raised again for our justification. (Romans 4.25)

Reconciled means coming into line with and accepting gladly God's will, purpose and control of my life.

Justified means excused from the *guilt of sin*. (See pages 103-4).

Saved includes saved from the *guilt and power of sin*, and *saved to a life of service and growing holiness*.

57

The Resurrection

The Cross is not the end; there follows the victory of the resurrection. What does it mean? Here was a creative act of God. *It was a new revelation of the living power of the living God.* We have learned that he is a God of righteousness, of purity, of truth—of righteousness and truth so unbending that Christ went to his Cross rather than give in to the forces of the world. We have learned that he is a God of love—of love to the uttermost, of love that forgives the vilest, of love that seeks to the very limit and goes on loving when everything seems hopeless. But Christ rose from the dead! *Here we learn that his Spirit of righteousness and love is also the secret of power, able to unlock the gates of death, and turn the forces of nature into instruments of his will.*

The resurrection has a meaning for life. *It means the possibility of new life here and now, a risen life, a new quality of being.* Life! Eternal life!

What manner of men is it not possible for us to be!

What manner of life is it not possible for us to live!

What manner of things is it not possible for us to do!

Christ has risen! No wonder the hymns about the resurrection resound with hallelujahs, for his resurrection brings to everyone the victory of God in life and in death.

New life! New joy! New hope!

[Thoughts based on *The Victory of God* by James Reid.]

The Last Week (Holy Week)

Palm Sunday	—a day of triumph	Mark 11.1-11
Monday	—a day of authority	Mark 11.12-19
Tuesday	—a day of conflict	Mark 11.20, 14.11
Wednesday	—not recorded in Mark	

Thursday	—a day with his disciples	Mark 14.12-31
Good Friday	—a day of suffering	Mark 14.32—15.47
Saturday		
Easter Sunday	—the resurrection day	Mark 16.1-13

Keep the Cross and resurrection in your mind all through this month. What does the Cross mean to me? What does it mean to the world?

> In the Cross of Christ I glory,
> Towering o'er the wrecks of time;
> All the light of sacred story
> Gathers round its head sublime.
>
> Sir John Bowring

Scripture Readings

The Deeper Training of the Disciples

Day	1	Mark 8.31, 9.1	Self-denial (the fellowship of his suffering)
	2	Mark 9.1-13	Transfiguration
	3	Mark 9.14-29	Prayer, the secret of power
	4	Mark 9.30-37	The greatness of humility
	5	Mark 9.38-50	Tolerance and strictness
	6	Mark 10.1-12	Marriage
	7	Mark 10.13-16	The value of a child and child-heart
	8	Mark 10.17-31	Riches of Christ (the Great Refusal)

On to Jerusalem

Day	9	Mark 10.32-34	'One who never turned his back'
	10	Mark 10.35-45	Ambition—servant of all is greatest of all
	11	Mark 10.46-52	Blind Bartimaeus—the blind see

Passion Week — The Last Week of Jesus' Life

Do you find reading pages 38-40 becoming too mechanical? If so, leave it for a few days, and on returning to it you should find that it comes to you with a greater freshness.

The Four Gospels

In the New Testament the first four books are stories of the life and teaching of Jesus. They differ in small details, but the main difference lies in the aspect of the life of Jesus that is emphasized.

Gospel	Emphasis	Jesus as	Written for
Matthew	Teaching	Messiah	Jewish Christians
Mark	Life	Man of action	Gentile Christians
Luke	Healing	Son of man	Gentile Christians
John	Spirit	Son of God	Christians

The word *Gentile* means anyone who is not a Jew.

Mark's Gospel: The Earliest Gospel

See pages 51-2.

Matthew's Gospel: For Jewish Christians

One big difference between this and the earliest Gospel is that Mark's principal interest is in the events of Jesus' life, while Matthew's is in his teaching. Early Christian tradition has it that Matthew, the disciple, took notes from time to time of the conversations and teaching of his Master and that these form the basis of the Gospel that bears his name. It is specially a Gospel for Jewish Christians. In this respect note the frequency of Old Testament quotations, the emphasis on the law and the Jewish messianic hope.

Matthew tells the story of his conversion in a single verse (9.9). Nor is any effort made to hide the depth from which Christ had lifted him: he was a tax gatherer, a man socially ostracized, for he had sold country and conscience, and probably character too, in a profession which every loyal

Jew branded as dishonourable. May not the writing of his Gospel to the Jews be his restitution for his former betrayal?

Luke's Gospel: For Gentile Christians

Luke is the one evangelist who was not a Jew. Christ is portrayed not primarily as the Messiah of Israel but *as the Saviour of the world*. Luke takes the story away from the local setting in Palestine and puts it in the framework of world history. He traces Jesus right back to Adam as the founder of the race and not to Abraham, the founder of Israel. He chooses incidents which show Jesus' missionary spirit and universal hope. Note the Good Samaritan, the grateful leper, and verses like Luke 13.29. In a pagan world, women and children are of little account. Luke emphasizes the tender, thoughtful, kindly attitude of Jesus to them.

Luke, who also wrote the Acts of the Apostles, was a doctor, a travelling companion of Paul's. He is sometimes called the Beloved Physician (Colossians 4.14). His training as a doctor also accounts for the special place he gives in this Gospel to the healing miracles of Jesus.

John's Gospel: The Last Gospel

This Gospel is, in some ways, different from the other three. It does not attempt to tell the story of the life of Jesus. It takes for granted a knowledge of the other Gospels and sets about supplementing their narratives by giving a deeper spiritual meaning of the work and person of Jesus. It was the last Gospel to appear. The thought, brooding, and spiritual communion of a lifetime have gone into its composition. It gives no parables. It concentrates on the Judean ministry of Jesus. Half of the Gospel has to do with the last week of Jesus' life. *It emphasizes Jesus as the Son of*

God. As to its author, the view can be strongly supported that it consists partly of reminiscences of the 'disciple whom Jesus loved', and partly of addresses on the life of Jesus subsequently preached by this disciple in Ephesus. This glorious fourth Gospel has made our picture of Jesus, the Son of God, more complete.

GOD'S MORAL LAW

The Law and Sin

The record of God's revelation is contained in the Scriptures. And the summary of his moral law can be found in the Ten Commandments given to the nation of Israel through Moses (Exodus 19). These Old Testament commandments are summarized in the New Testament by Jesus:

> Jesus said unto him, Thou shalt love the Lord thy God with all thy heart, and with all thy soul, and with all thy mind. This is the first and great commandment. And the second is like unto it, Thou shalt love thy neighbour as thyself. On these two commandments hang all the law and the prophets. (Matthew 22.37-40).

The catechism helps us to understand how God's moral law affects our lives today.

What do you learn in the Commandments?
I learn two things: my duty towards God, and my duty towards my neighbour.
What is your duty towards God?
My duty towards God is to believe in him, to reverence him, and to love him with all my heart, with all my mind, with all my soul, and with all my strength; to worship him; to give him thanks; to put my whole trust in him; to call upon him; to honour his Holy Name and his Word; and to serve him truly all the days of my life.
What is your duty towards your neighbour?

My duty towards my neighbour is to love him as myself, and to do to all men as I would they should do unto me: to love, honour and succour my father and mother: To honour and obey those in authority: To submit myself to all my governors, teachers, spiritual pastors and masters: To conduct myself humbly and reverently to all my betters: To hurt nobody by word or deed: To be true and just in all my dealings: To bear no malice or hatred in my heart: To keep my hands from stealing and my tongue from evil speaking, lying, and slandering: To keep my body in temperance, soberness, and chastity: Not to covet or desire other men's goods; but to serve and labour truly to get my own living, unto which it shall please God to call me.

Paul said, 'The law was our schoolmaster to bring us unto Christ, that we might be justified by faith.' With the law comes the conviction of sin.

What is sin? Would you accept these definitions?

Sin is rebellion against God. *I* do what *I* want. It is the attitude of 'My will not thine be done.' Therefore, God asks the surrender of my will.

Sin is anything we know we should do but won't or don't do. It is therefore disobedience. It is anything we know we should not do but do.

Sin is anything that separates me from God or another person. It includes attitudes like: pride, side, snobbishness, envy, spite, anger, hatred, selfishness. Therefore God asks the surrender of these attitudes.

Sin is coming short. It includes thoughtlessness about others, laziness in its relation to ourselves or others, and all those shortcomings which we so easily excuse in ourselves but condemn in others.

Sin is anything that is not of faith; that is, it is anything I cannot *fully justify to my conscience.*

I find the Four Absolute Standards given by the Oxford Group very helpful in clarifying the meaning of sin and the spirit of the law as given in the Sermon on the Mount.

Absolute Honesty. Absolute Purity.
Absolute Unselfishness. Absolute Love.

The Sermon on the Mount

Danger! Here comes the Sermon on the Mount. Danger!

We will be reading the Sermon on the Mount in Matthew's Gospel during the next few days—and there are at least three dangers to be faced as we read.

Danger 1. It shows up my failings.

Danger 2. People say it won't work.

Danger 3. I feel scared to try it.

How Should a Christian React to the Sermon on the Mount?

I have come to the conclusion that what we call the Sermon on the Mount is the way a Christian will act, that it constitutes the technique of being a Christian—it is his working philosophy of life . . .

Are the principles laid down in the Sermon on the Mount foreign laws? . . . Chesterton says that at first reading you feel that it turns everything upside down, but the second time you read it you discover that it turns everything right side up. The first time you read it you feel that it is impossible, but the second time, you feel that nothing else is possible. . . .

The Sermon on the Mount may seem impossible, but only in our worst moments. In our highest moments—that is, in our real moments—we feel that everything else is unbelievably impossible, an absurdity. (From *The Christ of the Mount* by E. Stanley Jones)

Let us make this part of our creed: '*I believe in the Sermon on the Mount and in its way of life, and I intend, God helping me, to embody it in my life.*'

Danger 1. It shows up my failings. Good. For a wise man to know his weaknesses is the first step towards conquering them.

Danger 2. People say it won't work. Have they tried it? Let me try it first. Jesus lived it.

Danger 3. I feel scared to try it. Faith casts feeling (fear) aside and launches out trusting in God's help. 'Fear not, only believe.' As for me, I make the plunge.

Read the Sermon on the Mount over and over again. Ponder its meaning; apply it to your daily life. Do not hedge or try to explain it away. Do not dilute its meaning but face its challenge. *Discover—or rediscover—it as a practical way of living.*

Scripture Readings

As you ponder over the passages, keep the three words *faith, love,* and *obedience* constantly before you. 'And this is his commandment, That we should *believe* on the name of his Son Jesus Christ, and love one another . . . And he that keepeth his commandments dwelleth in him, and he in him. And hereby we know that he abideth in us, by the Spirit which he hath given us' (1 John 3.23-24).

God's Moral Law

Day   1   Exodus 20.1-17   The Ten Commandments

The Spirit of the Law

Day	2	Micah 6.6-8	Righteousness, mercy, humility
	3	Psalm 51.10-19	A contrite and broken spirit
	4	Matthew 9.8-13	Mercy not sacrifice
	5	Luke 6.1-10	The spirit, not the letter of the law
	6	Luke 10.25-37	Love God and love your neighbour
	7	Luke 18.18-27	God must come first
	8	Psalm 119.1-16	Blessed are those who obey God's law

The Sermon on the Mount — The Ideal Character

Day	9	Matthew 5.1-5	Humble, penitent, thoughtful, meek
	10	Matthew 5.6-8	Upright, merciful, pure
	11	Matthew 5.9-12	Peacemaker, enduring persecution gladly
	12	Matthew 5.48	Perfect

Responsibility

Day	13	Matthew 5.13-16	Salt and light to the world

The Law and Its Spirit

Day	14	Matthew 5.17-20	Eternal value of God's law
	15	Matthew 5.21-26	Anger
	16	Matthew 5.27-32	Purity
	17	Matthew 5.33-37	Truth
	18	Matthew 5.38-48	Love

Why We Fail — Divided Loyalty

Day	19	Matthew 6.1-4	In charity
	20	Matthew 6.5-15	In praying
	21	Matthew 6.16-18	In fasting
	22	Matthew 6.19-23	In treasures
	23	Matthew 6.24-34	In worship and worry
	24	Matthew 7.1-6	In criticism

The Solution

Day	25	Matthew 6.33	One dominant purpose

God's Help to Reach This Ideal
Day 26 Matthew 7.7-11 The Holy Spirit (Luke 11.13)

Men's Work to Reach This Ideal
Day 27 Matthew 7.12-14 The golden rule and discipline

The Fruits Show the Roots
Day 28 Matthew 7.15-20 A warning

True Foundations
Day 29 Matthew 7.21-23 Doing God's will
     30 Matthew 7.24-29 Do. To know is not enough

Read *The Christ of the Mount* by E. Stanley Jones. As you read the passages this month have pages 28-9, and 33-7, constantly before you. They may help to give content to your readings.

The Ideal Character (The Beatitudes)

In the eight statements beginning with the word *blessed* in Matthew 5.1-12, Jesus gives us a description of the ideal character—someone who is like Jesus himself.

Poor in Spirit

This does not necessarily mean poor financially. It does mean:

- Humble towards God, prepared to own its sin, its dependence on God.
- Humble towards other people. Prepared to own its faults and make apology and restitution where necessary.
- Renounced in spirit. It seeks to know and do God's will.
- Patient. It will not stop short of its purpose.

- Content, not always getting tangled up in money and possessions. Not grumbling or discontented.

Mourning

- Repentant. It feels its own unworthiness.
- It feels the sorrows of others and longs to ameliorate them.

Meek

- It has all the passions of others, anger, fear, frustration, etc., *but it has them under control*. It is not their slave.
- It makes decisions according to faith and not according to fear. This is how the word *meek* is always used in the Bible. It is not cowed by other people's desires but seeks to please God.

Righteous

See the notes on 'Righteousness' on pages 33-4.

Merciful

See the notes on 'Love' on pages 34-5.

Pure

- Pure in speech. Pure in body. Pure in habits. This does not mean crushing the instincts but having the instincts as servant and not master of the spirit.
- Pure in outlook towards the opposite sex.
- Pure in mind and thought. For some people this means cutting out of their lives things that are quite legitimate for others.
- The temptation of impurity cannot be fought on one battlefield alone. It is intimately connected with lack

of discipline, laziness, self-indulgence in food, sleep, and habits. If you let the body master you in some things, it will tend to be master in everything. *Self-discipline is essential in the Christian life.*

Peacemakers

- It seeks harmony between man and God.
- It seeks to overcome by every Christian method within its power all that causes barriers between man and man, nation and nation.
- It seeks peace and goodwill among all men.

Persecuted

- For *righteousness* sake, for *my* (*Jesus'*) sake.
- Jesus took for granted that a life with the above character would be persecuted. The world is not willing to face the challenge of such a life. It wants only an average character. Those below, it puts in prison; those above, it persecutes and rejects.
- The only way to face persecution is to rejoice. Any other way of facing it fails to come out victorious. The apostles rejoiced 'that they were counted worthy to suffer shame for his name' (Acts 5.41).

This is the victorious character that overcomes all difficulties and triumphs over all circumstances. 'Be ye therefore perfect, even as your Father which is in heaven is perfect' (Matthew 5.48).

THE CHARACTER OF JESUS

Jesus, Our Example

The life of Jesus is the most beautiful there has ever been. One would have thought people would be naturally attracted by it, but attractiveness is not the only virtue of real goodness; it challenges.

The challenge of Jesus' life was too great. The people saw by comparison how much of their goodness was only outward show, it was only skin deep. They were too petty to answer that challenge. They crucified him instead.

Have a great aim—have a high standard—make Jesus your ideal. Be like him in character. Be like him in outlook and attitude towards God and man. Be like him in the home—thoughtful, patient, loving. Be like him in your work—honest, reliable, always willing to 'go the second mile'. Be like him in your social life—approachable, unselfish, considerate. Make him an ideal not merely to be admired but also to be followed.

The life of Jesus illustrates nearly every variety of true character. Humility, gentleness, patience, sympathy, charity, courage—all are blended together in that one personality.

The crowd gathered round him, for he spoke with authority, and not like the scribes. The people wondered at the gracious words that proceeded out of his mouth. Here is that unity of gentleness and power that stamps a really great character.

He entered the homes of the social outcasts without any snobbishness or pretension. He was known as the friend of publicans and sinners.

Courage and love, perfectly blended, were characteristic of his whole life. *He sought God's will and fearlessly followed it, no matter what the cost.* In his outlook towards people and his treatment of them, sympathy and love found expression in a practical way.

Allow the beauty of this character to absorb your thoughts so that whenever you deviate from his ideal, your conscience will convict you. When that happens, do not try to excuse yourself. Face your fault. Own it to be yours and yours alone. Ask God's forgiveness and where it affects others, ask their forgiveness too. Ask God's Spirit to stand by you and help you till that part of your character, outlook, or attitude comes into line with the ideal you have in Jesus.

Jesus as Lord

To speak of Jesus as Lord means that I give him the control of my will. As a lord can dictate to his servant saying, 'Do this', 'Do that', and the servant's duty is to obey, even so it is with me.

I say 'Lord Jesus', meaning Jesus is now Lord of my life to lead and dictate. My greatest joy is just to do what pleases him.

'Lord, what wilt thou have me to do?' says Paul when he is confronted by the living Christ (Acts 9.6). He looked for orders from his new Lord.

'I heard the voice of the Lord, saying, Whom shall I send, and who will go for us? Then said I [Isaiah], Here am I, send me' (Isaiah 6.8).

'Not my will but thine,' says Jesus in Gethsemane. That is what Lordship means, not my will but God's. Am I prepared to launch out on this basis, surrendering my will?

Jesus as Saviour

Jesus as example makes me very conscious of my faults, my shortcomings, my sins, my weakness, and my failure to conform to that ideal. My mind agrees with the ideal, but my will does not respond to it.

'Miserable wretch that I am! Who will rescue me from this body of death? God will! Thanks be to him through Jesus Christ our Lord.' (Romans 7.24-5, Moffat). This is the gospel, the Good News.

I find I need more than an ideal: I need a Saviour to save me from the *guilt of sin*; to save me from the *power of sin*. I need a Saviour whose *grace is sufficient to enable me to live a life of unselfish service and love.*

Behold the Lamb of God, which taketh away the sin of the world. (John 1.29)

Thou shalt call his name Jesus: for he shall save his people from their sins. (Matthew 1.21)

There is none other name under heaven given among men, whereby we must be saved. (Acts 4.12)

> My faith looks up to thee
> Thou Lamb of Calvary,
>   Saviour divine!
> Now hear me while I pray,
> Take all my guilt away,
> O let me from this day
>   Be wholly thine!
>
> May thy rich grace impart
> Strength to my fainting heart,
>   My zeal inspire;
> As thou hast died for me,

O may my love to thee
Pure, warm, and changeless be,
    A living fire!

Ray Palmer

Scripture Readings

These readings are short ones. Read them over carefully and prayerfully. Spend some time asking yourself what they mean for you today, under your circumstances. Is there any challenge to your character, outlook, or attitudes to God or man? If so, are you prepared to face it?

Jesus, Our Example

Day		
1	Matthew 4.1-11	The refusal to compromise
2	Mark 1.32-37	Jesus and prayer
3	John 16.25-37	Serenity
4	Luke 4.16-30	Wider horizons; vision
5	Matthew 8.1-4	Sympathy
6	Matthew 14.13-21	Patience
7	Mark 10.13-16	Gentle Jesus
8	Mark 3.1-6	Indignation
9	John 2.13-17	Moral courage
10	Luke 19.1-10	Appreciativeness
11	John 8.1-11	Charity of outlook
12	Luke 12.13-21	Doing without
13	Matthew 20.20-28	Duty; God's will
14	Luke 5.27-32	Jesus, the brother of man
15	Matthew 22.15-22	Citizenship
16	John 13.1-17	Humility
17	John 18.33-38	Truthfulness

Jesus, Lord and Saviour

Day	18	Luke 5.17-26	He saves by forgiving sin
	19	John 8.1-11	He saves by sympathy
	20	John 19.25-30	'It is finished.' What?
	21	2 Corinthians 5.14-21	Reconciled to God
	22	Ephesians 2.1-10	Saved by grace
	23	Ephesians 2.11-22	Peace with God
	24	1 John 1.3-10	Cleansed by his blood
	25	Acts 4.5-12	Salvation in one Name only
	26	1 Corinthians 1.17-24	The cross—the power of God
	27	1 Corinthians 2.1-5	Jesus Christ and him crucified

Surrender—Dedication

Day	28	Luke 9.57-62	The price of discipleship
	29	Luke 9.23-27	The price of discipleship
	30	Matthew 10.32-39	The price of discipleship
	31	John 15.10-21	The price of discipleship

Read the piece on surrender that follows, and, 'How do I surrender?' on pages 31-2. Does God ask of you a more complete surrender than you have been prepared to make up to the present? If so, are you willing to make that surrender now?

Surrender

William James says, 'The crisis of self-surrender has always been, and must always be, regarded as the vital turning point of the religious life.' That is why I am asking you to surrender your life to God.

You know God's law, God's purpose for the world, the life of Jesus, the meaning of sin, God's sacrifice for man's sin and his offer of forgiveness. *It is not more knowledge that you need, but a decision you must make.* Are you willing to accept God's gracious offer of forgiveness and surrender your life to him, *coming under his control* and dedicating yourself to his service?

God's will is only revealed to us step by step. He reveals more as we obey what we know. Surrender means that we are prepared to follow his will step by step as it is revealed to us, no matter what the cost.

The glorious offer of the New Testament is that of a transforming, communicable sense of the power and presence of God. It is an experience characterized by the liberating sense of forgiveness and offered to everyone, an experience that changes life, and an experience which we want to pass on to others. Christ's parables, in the main, are concerned with the passionate desire of God that we should be brought into this experience . . .

Paul's metaphors are nearly all employed with the same end in view. Something happens in the human soul which is done by God; which man, of himself, cannot achieve . . .

The message of the New Testament is that the most important thing in the world is that we should get our relationship right with God and receive this transforming experience. No hereditary Christianity . . . is a substitute for it. No doing good to others, no life dedicated to the service of humanity or passed in what men call 'playing the game' will do. Men often say to us: 'I don't see what religion matters as long as we are doing good and paying our way and being kind and loving and living a moral life. That is surely all God demands.' *The point is not what God demands, but what Christ offers.* (From *Discipleship* by Leslie D. Weatherhead)

Surrender is taking my hands off and letting God forgive, cleanse, or in some way act so as to meet my personal need. Surrender is our side of giving God a chance to show us what keeps us from receiving this experience of accepting Christ's offer, here and now, of abundant life. Life—full, free, joyous, and contentedly serene. (Reread pages 29-30 on 'What Do I Surrender?' and pages 31-2 on 'How Do I Surrender?')

THE KINGDOM OF GOD— THE KINGDOM OF HEAVEN

The central idea and commonest phrase of the preaching of Jesus was 'the kingdom of God', which Matthew translates as 'the kingdom of heaven'. Jesus did not invent the phrase. It was an historical one, handed down from the past, and was common in the mouths of his contemporaries. John the Baptist's message was 'Repent, for the kingdom of God is at hand.'

Jesus Told Us the Kingdom Was Already in Existence

Note the form in which he bids us to pray for it:

Thy kingdom come

Thy will be done } in earth as it is in heaven

That is, we pray for the kingdom as it already exists in heaven. 'Which brings at once the stirring thought so easily ignored in the materialism of earth-life, that this kingdom is already existing with all its powers and all its laws' in the spiritual world from which Jesus came. Jesus is only founding a colony on earth of the already existing kingdom in heaven. The apostle Paul told the Christians at Philippi that they were a colony of heaven (see Philippians 3.20).

[Thoughts based on *A People's Life of Christ* by J. Paterson-Smyth]

The Kingdom of God is Righteousness, and Peace, and Joy in the Holy Spirit
(Romans 14.17)

It is by personal knowledge of Christ that we become citizens in this kingdom, and that privilege is open to all. The humblest and most obscure may have direct personal communion with Christ through the Holy Spirit. Indeed, every one of us must have such personal knowledge if we are to be citizens of the kingdom.

The laws of the kingdom concern the hearts of men, their thoughts and desires, their motives and imaginations, as well as the outward acts in which those issue.

The rule of Christ is never imposed, and is never sustained, by any kind of violence. Christ wins men into his kingdom, and holds them there by the power of his goodness and love.

The Kingdom of God is Personal

'The kingdom of God is within you.' The reign of God in me is letting God take control of my life, so that this day, and each day, I live to please God. Nothing more, nothing less. I make his laws my laws; his will my will; his outlook my outlook. No longer do I make decisions on the old basis of selfishness, ease, pleasure, or personal desire but on the new basis of righteousness, truth, and love. Is it the kind of thing Jesus would say or do? If so, go ahead, for by so doing the kingdom of God comes a little nearer to being realized here on earth.

The Kingdom of God is Worldwide

The kingdom of God is a new order founded on the fatherly love of God, on redemption, justice, and brotherhood. It is meant to enter into all life, all nations, and all policies till the kingdoms of this world become the kingdom of our Lord. It is no use having vague ideas about this. We must determine that as far as we are concerned, by the help of the Spirit of God, we intend to live for this kingdom and in the spirit of it.

It was Christ's Lofty Vision to Make a Beautiful World

It was a vision far off of a nobler humanity, of Courage and Heroism, of Righteousness and Love, of true men and pure women, of kindly hearts and helpful hands, of Knights of God going out to sweep oppression from the earth, to pull the poor sinful world straight. It was Jesus' vision of a Golden Age on earth, a Kingdom where a righteous, loving God should rule and where men should by love serve one another.

Let the sweet, fair vision rise before you. Christ's ideal for His Church. *A band of loyal hearts* following Him for love of Him, walking through this world ennobling life, then trustfully stepping out with Him off the edge of the world into the thrilling adventure of the Hereafter. Of all the romantic expeditions which this world has seen, there is none more romantic than this to which Jesus called men by the Galilean lake long ago, and to which He is calling them . . . today. (From *A People's Life of Christ* by J. Paterson-Smyth, italics added)

As regards this kingdom, where do I stand? Can I say:

> Just as I am, young, strong and free,
>   To be the best that I can be
> For truth, and righteousness, and Thee,
>   Lord of my life, I come.
>
> M. Farningham (d. 1909)

What am I Doing to Bring in this Kingdom?

What am I doing to combat the ignorance, prejudice, and sin in the world? What am I doing to uplift, enrich, and ennoble life? God has some work for me to do. It may never be done unless I launch out fearlessly to do it.

That work is most likely at your very doorstep, in your home, your school, your church, your town. (How many people in your town cannot read or write? What are you doing about it?) Or it may be among your friends.

'Father, open thou mine eyes that I may see.'

Scripture Readings

These readings are short ones. Read them over. Spend a few minutes asking yourself what they mean for you today, under your circumstances. 'What doth the Lord require of thee, but to do justly [righteousness], and to love mercy [love], and to walk humbly with thy God [humility]?' (Micah 6.8)

Entrance to the Kingdom

Day			
	1	Matthew 4.12-17	Repentance
	2	John 3.1-17	The new birth
	3	Matthew 18.1-6	Childlike humility

The Laws of the Kingdom

Day			
	4	Matthew 5.21-26	Anger
	5	Matthew 5.27-32	Purity
	6	Matthew 5.33-37	Sincerity
	7	Luke 10.25-28	Love to God
	8	Luke 10.29-36	Love to your neighbour
	9	Matthew 5.38-48	Love to your enemy
	10	1 Corinthians 13.1-8a	Love defined

Parables of the Kingdom

Day	11	Matthew 13.1-9	Hindrances
	12	Matthew 13.10-17	What makes us dull to understand?
	13	Matthew 13.24-30	Enemies of the kingdom
	14	Matthew 13.31-35	The growth of the kingdom
	15	Matthew 13.14-46	The value of the kingdom

The Kingdom

Day	16	Matthew 6.24-34	One dominant purpose
	17	Romans 14.1-17	Righteousness, peace, and joy
	18	Matthew 9.10-13	No class distinction
	19	Acts 10.34-38	No race distinction
	20	Acts 8.26-38	No colour distinction

Children of the Kingdom

Day	21	Matthew 12.46-50	Those who do God's will
	22	Matthew 7.21-29	Action not words
	23	Romans 8.1-11	Those in whom the Holy Spirit dwells
	24	Romans 8.12-17	Those led by the Spirit
	25	1 John 4.1-6	Those who believe in Jesus
	26	1 John 4.8-21	Those who love the brethren
	27	John 1.6-14	Those who receive Jesus
	28	1 John 3.1-11	Those who act righteously

The Final Tests

Day	29	Matthew 25.14-30	Faith and faithfulness in action
	30	Matthew 25.31-46	Love in action

The New Birth—Regeneration

Christianity is not discipline, though discipline will enter into it.

Christianity is not morality, but the moral laws will be followed.

Christianity is not following a great example, but this will be done.

Christianity is not living by laws or rules; it is living by grace.

True Christianity starts with the new birth. 'Ye must be born again' (John 3.7).

The new birth is God coming into your life and giving you a new nature, a nature of love to God and man. Nothing in life can make up for the lack of this; nothing can take its place.

'Though I have the gift of prophecy, and understand all mysteries, and all knowledge; and though I have all faith, so that I could remove mountains, and have not charity, I am nothing. And though I bestow all my goods to feed the poor, and though I give my body to be burned, and have not charity, it profiteth me nothing' (1 Corinthians 13.2-3). Without love (God), I am nothing. 'Marvel not that I said unto thee, Ye must be born again' (John 3.7).

If any doctrines within the whole compass of Christianity may be termed 'fundamental', they are doubtless these two: . . . justification . . . relating to that great work which God does *for us*, in forgiving our sins . . . the new birth . . . relating to the great work which God does *in us*, in renewing our fallen nature . . .

[The New Birth] is *that great change which God works* in the soul when He brings it into life; when He raises it from the death of sin to the life of righteousness. It is the change wrought in the soul by the almighty Spirit of God when it is 'created anew in Christ Jesus'; when it is 'renewed after the image of God in righteousness and true holiness'; when the love of the world is changed into the love of God: pride into humility; passion into meekness; hatred, envy, malice, into a sincere, tender, disinterested love for all mankind. (From a Sermon by John Wesley)

New Life—The Dynamic for Living

Christian living is made possible by the new birth. You never can understand the meaning of Christian living until God comes into your life. Christian living is bound up with Christian faith; personal faith in God, which brings his power into your life. It is not by mere commandments that a Christian lives, but by a new spirit in his heart. Goodness comes, not as a result of laws and rules, but as a 'fruit of the Spirit'. It is not by 'laws' or 'works' but by 'grace'. It is not I, but the grace of God which was with me. The grace of God is his wonderful free love coming into our hearts through faith in Jesus Christ. When it comes it changes everything. With some it comes suddenly, with others gradually. But when God enters our lives in this way we begin to live (we are born again). People describe it in different ways, but all say that new life has come to them. 'To you also, who were dead through your offences and sins, . . . God has given life' (Ephesians 2.1-2, Weymouth).

This is the message of Jesus—'new life'. Go tell the world, 'the deaf hear', 'the blind see', 'the dead are raised up'.

GOD IS LOVE

Herein is love, not that we loved God, but that he loved us, and sent his Son to be the propitiation for our sins. (1 John 4.10)

God is love is the most complete statement of what God is like. Love is part of every other attribute of God. There are many things like pain, sickness, natural calamity, undeserved suffering, wars and death which make many people ask, 'How can such things be if the world is ruled by a God who is absolutely good?'

The Source of Love

God is the source of all love. He is love itself. But we could never have understood this had he not revealed himself as love through Jesus offering the perfect sacrifice of himself for us. So love begins from God's side. 'Love is not something which belongs to human nature or starts from our side towards God. It is all the other way.'

We need to meditate on this great truth, 'God is love', until it becomes the heart of all our thinking and living. There at the centre of the universe, the sustaining life of all things, is One who feels and wills and suffers and loves.

I cannot prove that God is love. Gradually, as we meditate on it and allow its implications to be put into practice, life finds a new meaning and purpose; work has a new incentive; life's tragedies are faced in a new spirit (the cross was no problem to Jesus as regards the love of God); people take on a new attractiveness; we begin to see in them unsuspected beauty of character and new possibilities. *Love is the key that brings sense and meaning into the world.* And, after all, *is not this the greatest proof that it is true?* Where love is, God is. I see it; I feel it; I know it: 'We love, because he first loved us.'

> For God so loved the world that he gave his only begotten son, that whosoever believeth in him should not perish, but have everlasting life. (John 3.16)

> When God loves, he loves the world.
> When God gives, he gives his Son.
> When God invites, he invites everybody.
> When God saves, he saves everlastingly.

God's love is like a lake in the eternal hills. The gift of his Son is like a river flowing forth from that lake. Our faith is like a pitcher that draws soul-reviving, thirst-quenching, life-giving draughts from this river of love and life.

[Thoughts largely taken from the Bible Reading Fellowship Notes of January 13, 1939, and November 14, 1940.]

> Thou shalt love the Lord the God with all thy *heart*, and with all thy *soul*, and with all thy *strength*, and with all thy *mind*. (Luke 10.27, italics added)

> Thou shalt love thy neighbour as thyself. (Mark 12.31)

The Spectrum of Love

Patience	'Love suffereth long.'
Kindness	'And is kind.'
Generosity	'Love envieth not.'
Humility	'Love vaunteth not itself, is not puffed up.'
Courtesy	'Doth not behave itself unseemly.'

Unselfishness	'Seeketh not its own.'
Good Temper	'Is not easily provoked.'
Guilelessness	'Thinketh no evil.'
Sincerity	'Rejoiceth not in iniquity but rejoiceth in the truth.'

In these few words from 1 Corinthians 13 we have what might be called the spectrum of love. Observe what its elements are. Notice that they have common names; that they are virtues which we hear about every day; that they are things which can be practised by every man in every place in life; and how by a multitude of small things and ordinary virtues, the supreme good is made up.

Patience, kindness, generosity, humility, courtesy, unselfishness, good temper, guilelessness, sincerity—these make up the supreme gift, the stature of the perfect man.

You will observe that all are in relation to man, in relation to life, in relation to the known today and the near tomorrow, and not to the unknown eternity.

We hear much of love to God; Christ spoke much of love to man.

We make a great deal of peace with heaven; Christ made much of peace on earth. Religion is not a strange or added thing, but the inspiration of the secular life, the breathing of an eternal spirit through this temporal world.

The supreme thing, in short, is not a thing at all, but *the giving of a further finish to the multitudinous words and acts which make up the sum of every common day.* (From *The Greatest Thing in the World* by Henry Drummond)

If a man say, I love God, and hateth his brother, he is a liar; for he that loveth not his brother whom he hath seen, how can he love God whom he hath not seen? . . . He who loveth God loves his brother also. (1 John 4.20-21)

Scripture Readings

Again this month the readings are short ones. Read them over. Spend a few minutes asking yourself what they mean for you today, under your circumstances.

> We love, because he first loved us. (1 John 4.19, RV)
> So God created man in his own image. (Loving and righteous; (Genesis 1.27)

> Clothe yourselves with that new and better self which has been created to resemble God in the righteousness and holiness of the truth. (Ephesians 4.24, Weymouth)

The Love of God — Ways in Which It Is Shown

Day		
1	Psalm 8.1-9	In his not forgetting, in the power he gives us
2	Acts 17.22-31	In his patience with man
3	Psalm 23.1-6	In his protection
4	Psalm 103.1-14	In his grace and mercy
5	Matthew 5.43-48	In his love for all, good or evil
6	Matthew 6.25-34	In his dependability
7	John 3.14-18	In his sacrifice
8	Philippians 2.5-11	In his humility and obedience
9	Luke 15.11-24	In his genuine joy
10	Romans 5.6-11	In his initiative in redemption
11	John 1.1-14	In his method of redemption
12	Romans 3.20-26	In his method of justification
13	Luke 19.1-10	In his identification with sinners
14	Luke 15.1-10	In the value he places on us
15	Ephesians 1.3-11	In the place he has for us in his world purpose
16	Ephesians 2.1-10	In the change he makes in our lives
17	Titus 3.3-7	In the change he makes in our lives
18	Galatians 4.1-7	In giving us the gift of sonship

The Love of God—Its Implications or Results

Badge of Discipleship

During the readings this month keep pages 34-6 on 'Love' constantly before you. This is the meaning of love in the Christian sense.

The Christian Home

A happy Christian home is a glory to God, a challenge and example to man and a tower of strength to the nation. The home should be the place we automatically think of, and turn to, for fellowship, understanding, joy, and rest.

One of the results of true religion should be a happy home life.

The Foundations of the Christian Home

God

One foundation of the Christian home is a practical faith in God that brings all—the daily routine, the daily work, the future plans, the problems of the children, everything—before God, and seeks wisdom to know and courage to do, his will. This is building one's home with God at the centre, or allowing God to build the home. 'Except the Lord build the house, they labour in vain that build it' (Psalm 127.1). God is the Head of this home, the Dictator in all actions, the Guide in all difficulties and the Friend at all times. *Ask his wisdom; seek his guidance; follow his plan.*

If you lack wisdom to build a home like this, ask God who giveth liberally to all. (See James 1.5.)

Parents, 'provoke not your children to wrath'—do not have a nagging attitude towards them that creates irritation, but bring them up to know God—teach them about him and lead them into the way of living with him at the centre of their lives. (See Ephesians 6 and Colossians 3.)

Righteousness

One side of righteousness is filial piety; the other is its reciprocal, in which the parents respect the personality of the child. Christian homes are only happy if both these relationships are right. There should be transparent honesty, loyalty and trust between the members of the family. Nothing breaks up the joyous nature of a home so much as having to hide things from one another. Husband and wife should be able to face *everything* together, keeping nothing back. It is a sad day when this crystal clear relationship is broken. It is a sad day when a child has to hide anything from its parents. It is a sad day when the parents have to deceive their children or frighten them in order to gain their obedience.

There must be loyalty. Loyalty often demands courage. Stand by one another in difficulty, hardship and loss. Stand by one another when the world cheers, ridicules or neglects. Out of honesty and loyalty, trust grows. Trust and confidence is the environment that makes for happiness. Children, honour your parents with obedience. Parents, by transparent honesty, inspire your children to trust.

Love

Love is the essential element in the Christian home. Efficiency, cleanliness, luxury, cannot make up for the lack of love. Look up the meaning of love on pages 34-6. Love is interest in what the other members of the family do — joys and sorrows, struggles and achievements, are shared by all. Love anticipates. It sees beforehand how it can help to lighten another's load; it is always willing to go out of its way, or to make time, to help. Love never harbours resentment, is not easily hurt, is always ready to forgive. Where love is, God is.

Remember the marriage vow — the twofold, lifelong promise given. 'Wilt thou love, comfort, honour her [him], and keep her [him], in sickness and in health; and forsaking all others keep thee only unto her [him] so long as ye both shall live?' '*I will.*'

Ask yourself, 'Am I keeping this promise in the letter and in the spirit?' When love is dethroned and the relationship is wrong at the centre, how can the home be happy? Love is the secret of a happy home.

God — righteousness — love — loyalty
are foundations for a Christian home.

THE LIFE OF PAUL—
THE ACTS OF THE APOSTLES

This month we will read about the spread of the gospel through the Roman world as recorded in the book of Acts. One of the major characters in Acts is the apostle Paul, who is also the author of thirteen letters of the New Testament.

Paul's life as a Christian apostle lasted some thirty years, but his missionary activities, as recorded by Luke in Acts, and all his Epistles belong to the last fifteen years.

What follows is a list of the outstanding events in Paul's life about which something should be known by everyone. The dates given are only approximate, as no one can speak with absolute authority concerning them.

Born about the same time as Jesus	
The crucifixion	AD 30
The conversion of Saul	33
The silent years	33-46
First missionary journey with Barnabas	47
Council at Jerusalem	49
Second missionary journey with Silas	49
Arrival at Corinth, spent 1½ years there	50
Third missionary journey up to Ephesus	52
Leaves Ephesus	55
Arrested at Jerusalem	56
Reaches Rome as a prisoner	59
Two years a prisoner with limited freedom	
End of the story in Acts	61
Death of Paul	Uncertain

The dates, places, and order of writing the Epistles cannot

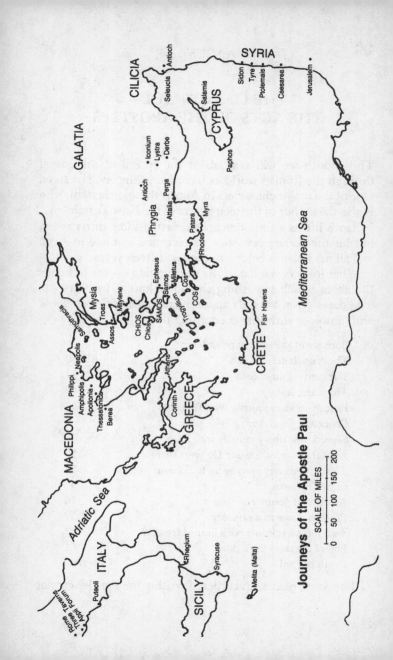

Journeys of the Apostle Paul

SCALE OF MILES

0   50   100 150 200

Journeys of the Apostle Paul

First Journey	*Second Journey*	*Third Journey*	*To Rome*
Antioch (Syria)	Antioch (Syria)	Antioch (Syria)	Sidon
Seleucia	Syria	Galatia	Myra
Salamis (Cyprus)	Cilicia	Phrygia	Fair Havens
Paphos	Derbe	Ephesus	Melita (Malta)
Perga	Lystra	Macedonia	Syracuse
Antioch (Pisidia)	Phrygia	Greece	Rhegium
Iconium	Galatia	Philippi	Puteoli
Lystra	Mysia	Troas	Appii Forum
Derbe	Troas	Assos	Three Taverns
Lystra	Samothracia	Mitylene	Rome
Iconium	Neapolis	Chios	
Antioch (Pisidia)	Philippi	Samos	
Perga	Amphipolis	Trogyllium	
Attalia	Appolonia	Miletus	
Antioch (Syria)	Thessalonia	Ephesus	
	Berea	Cos	
	Athens	Rhodes	
	Corinth	Patara	
	Ephesus	Tyre	
	Caesarea	Ptolemais	
	Antioch (Syria)	Caesarea	
		Jerusalem	

be given definitely in some cases, but there are two periods that are helpful to remember.

1. From his arrival in Corinth in AD 50 to his departure from Ephesus in AD 55, the following were probably written, perhaps in this order: 1 and 2 Thessalonians; 1 and 2 Corinthians; Galatians; Romans.

2. During Paul's period as a prisoner, some think in Rome, he wrote the Epistles of the Imprisonment—Ephesians, Philippians, Colossians and Philemon, and then the Pastoral Epistles of 1 and 2 Timothy and Titus. Whether or not these Pastoral Epistles are genuine letters of Paul has been much disputed. The traditional view is that they were written by Paul towards the end of his life. There are many arguments against this; none in themselves decisive but the cumulative effect is considerable. The thoughts in them are undoubtedly Pauline and could easily have come from his pen. The important thing, however, is that they are handed down to us by the Christian society whose experience has found in them a word from God.

The Council of Jerusalem—Acts 15.1-29

The religion of the Old Testament was the revelation of God through the individual Jew and through the Jewish nation. There had grown up with the religion, as part of it, many rites and ceremonies peculiarly Jewish.

Jesus came as a Saviour not only for the Jews, but for the whole world. Before long, as more Gentiles (those not Jews) became Christians, the question of how many of these rites and ceremonies were essential for them to observe became acute.

The question was so important for the whole future of Christianity that it could not be left to local churches to answer for themselves. A definite ruling was expected from the mother church at Jerusalem.

A council had been summoned to meet. Paul hurried back from his first missionary journey so as to give a report of the work of the Holy Spirit among the Gentiles and add to the discussion of this vital question.

It would appear that Paul in private conversations won over the church leaders in Jerusalem to his point of view. Then at the council meeting, after much discussion, a verdict was given in which we can see the guiding hand of God. Had the verdict been otherwise, Christianity would have ceased to be a missionary religion and would have been a Jewish sect and nothing more.

What is the Christian outlook on the question raised?

The answer is *equality* and *liberty*.

To understand the outlook on *equality*, it is best to read Acts 10.1-48. In the sight of God all are equal. 'God is no respecter of persons: But in every nation he that feareth him, and worketh righteousness, is accepted with him.' Because God is like this, therefore we should all meet in the same spirit of equality.

To understand the outlook on *liberty*, it is best to read Romans 14.1-23. The question of eating food given to idols is discussed here as it was pertinent at that time, but the general principle is the same for all questions. In things doubtful there should be liberty of conscience, *but if the conscience in any way convicts us then it is not of faith and therefore should not be done.* Or if an act causes a weaker person to stumble, we should be willing to refrain from it. The kingdom of God has primarily to do with righteousness, peace, and joy in the Holy Spirit, not outward form or ritual.

Christian liberty means freedom within the law of righteousness and love.

Christianity Advances into Europe—
Acts 16.6-10

This is a most important section. It records the entrance of Christianity into Europe. It marks a great day in the history of the world. God's call and God's guidance were very strong in directing the expansion of his kingdom. What tremendous issues depended upon obedience to that guidance!

Have you learned to hear God's voice saying, 'This is the way, walk ye in it?' Have you learned to obey? Do you realize the tremendous issues that may be at stake?

Scripture Readings

The readings are longer for this section in order to have the life of Paul brought before us in one month. Jot down the points that strike you while reading the story. Ponder over them. What can they mean to you? The Acts of the Apostles is the Gospel of the Holy Spirit. Give him time to reveal to your heart the message he has for you.

The Life of Paul—A Fellow Worker with God

Day	1	Acts 7.54-60	Enter Saul
	2	Acts 9.1-9	Conversion—the climax of an inner struggle
	3	Acts 9.10-22	God prepares both sides
	4	Acts 9.23-31	The past—a limitation and an asset

First Missionary Journey

Day	5	Acts 13.1-12	Cyprus, the home of Barnabas
	6	Acts 13.13-25	Pisidian Antioch; John Mark fails
	7	Acts 13.26-52	Opposition; filled with joy and the Holy Spirit

| 8 | Acts 14.1-7 | Iconium |
| 9 | Acts 14.8-28 | Lystra and Derbe; through affliction to the kingdom |

Council at Jerusalem
| Day | 10 | Acts 15.1-35 | Equality—liberty (see pages 96-7) |

Second Missionary Journey
Day	11	Acts 15.36—16.10	Galatia; Macedonia; guidance (see page 98)
	12	Acts 16.11-24	Philippi—Christianity and business
	13	Acts 16.25-30	Philippi—Christianity in prison surroundings
	14	Acts 17.1-15	Thessalonica; Athens; Christianity a revolution
	15	Acts 17.16-34	Athens—making the unknown known
	16	Acts 18.1-11	Corinth—man's view dim, God's clear
	17	Acts 18.12-22	Impartiality or indifference?

Third Missionary Journey
Day	18	Acts 18.23—19.10	Galatia, Phrygia, Ephesus—Christians lacking what?
	19	Acts 19.11-20	Christianity not a set formula
	20	Acts 19.21-41	Rationalizing; concern for God or business?
	21	Acts 20.1-16	Macedonia, Greece, Troas, Mitylene; visit to evangelize; onward; revisit to strengthen
	22	Acts 20.17-38	Farewell to Ephesus; drawn by love and duty
	23	Acts 21.1-40	Jerusalem, despite the danger
	24	Acts 22.1-30	Paul's wonderful story
	25	Acts 23.1-35	Beset on all sides, but strengthened by God
	26	Acts 24.1-27	On trial before Felix
	27	Acts 25.1-27	On trial before Festus, Paul appeals to Caesar

Paul's life summarized: 'For me to live is Christ' (Philippians 1.21).

As you read the story of Paul's journeys, follow him on the map on page 94.

THE EPISTLE TO THE ROMANS— PAUL'S GOSPEL

The Faith of Christ—a Faith for the World

The Epistle to the Romans is perhaps the greatest and most influential of all the letters of Paul. He wrote this letter from Corinth towards the end of his third missionary journey.

Paul had already occupied the strategic points of the ancient world for Christ: Antioch, Ephesus, Philippi, Corinth. But Rome was the centre of the Graeco-Roman world. To win Rome for Christ would be a victory the importance of which could not be overestimated. We can understand, therefore, the sense of urgency which made him say, 'After I have been there [Jerusalem], I must also see Rome' (Acts 19.21).

The church at Rome was of special importance and if he were to write a letter to it, the letter must be a special one. *Now was the occasion to put all his powers into a statement of the gospel such as he had never given before.*

Paul was at this time keenly sensible of the uncertainty of the future. He knew his life was in serious danger. (See Acts 20.3; 21.13.)

With this in mind, he may have made the letter *a statement in which he would leave behind him a full exposition of his faith*. It is a sustained treatment of one theme, *the greatness of the way of salvation through faith*.

Analysis of Romans

Justification
>—pronounced innocent, pardoned.
>—Christ's righteousness imputed to us.
>—God's work *for us* through his Son.

Sanctification
>—a cleansing from all sin.
>—a gradual process started at conversion.
>—God's work *in us* by his Spirit.

Election
>—This does not mean that some people are chosen by God to be saved and others to be damned. Election is God's choosing or doing anything in which *our merit or power* have no part. Those who believe become sons of God; they receive the Spirit of holiness to live as Christ lived. In 'election' *promise (privilege) and duty* go hand in hand. All God's free, unmerited gifts are such that *the final issue depends on our future obedience.*

> We are saved . . . to serve.
> God's promises imply . . . duties.
> Privileges carry . . . responsibilities.

Destiny is not determined by privilege but by our response to that privilege.

The Just shall Live by Faith—
Justification by Faith

Man has before him a choice between two ways of living. *He can live by law*, where righteousness comes by perfect obedience to that law. *He can live by faith*, where righteousness comes by grace on God's side, and by trust and confidence in Christ on our side.

The first brings two inescapable and insoluble difficulties.

1. Man's sense of sin—he has not lived in perfect obedience.
2. Man's sense of impotence—he cannot live such a life.

These facts we know from experience, but Paul brings another reason. We have inherited a nature too weak for the arduous attainment of righteousness: human nature is carnal now, not spiritual, and therefore unequal to the supreme spiritual achievement. The law could not alter this; *it had no creative power to change my nature*. On the contrary, it aggravated the evil. Its clear and full description of sins, which would have been a guide to a sound nature, actually multiplies offences. The very knowledge of sin tempts to its commission; the very command 'not to do' is a reason to a diseased nature for doing it. This was the effect of the law. *It is one thing to know the law and another to do it*, but it is doing, not knowing, which is righteousness.

God used the law, like a skilful physician, to bring my sore to a head in order that he might heal. The law was not a means of salvation, but only a means to show the need for salvation.

[Thoughts based on *The Life of St. Paul* by James Stalker]

'Miserable wretch that I am! Who will rescue me from this body of death?' God will! 'Thanks be to Him through Jesus Christ our Lord' (Romans 7.24-25, Moffatt).

This is the gospel (good news), that while I was unable to

find a way, God, in his mercy and grace, provided one. Man's extremity was God's opportunity.

Justification by faith was God's answer to man's great need.

Guilt

Man's sense of guilt God meets by forgiveness in Christ. Few things take from life so much of its interest and joy, so much of its confidence and power, as a sense of being in a wrong relationship with God, a sense of guilt with its accompanying fear, a sense of sin unforgiven.

Man reforms his ways to *seek* forgiveness.

Man does meritorious acts to *earn* forgiveness.

Man turns to penance and prayer to *purchase* forgiveness.

But there is a life of conscious forgiveness, with all the liberating effects that forgiveness brings, and this life is the gift of grace, and carries with it only one human condition— faith.

By grace are ye saved, through faith; and that not of yourselves: it is the gift of God. (Ephesians 2.8)

Being justified freely by his grace through the redemption that is in Christ Jesus: Whom God hath set forth to be a propitiation *through faith in his blood*, to declare his righteousness for the remission of sins that are past. (Romans 3.24-25, italics added)

Impotence

Man's sense of impotence God meets with his power. To live this life that is pleasing to God demands faith daily to appropriate God's power (God's righteousness), or better to allow God's power to flow into, and work through, our lives. This power comes into our lives as we live faith moment by moment. 'The just shall live by faith' (Romans 1.17).

Scripture Readings

The readings for this month cover what formed the basic thinking of Paul. It is well worth spending as much time as we can spare to meditate on the passages for each day till the truths they contain become part of ourselves—*moulding our outlook and attitudes, determining our actions, and shaping our judgements*. In this way harmony is obtained between our mental outlook and our practical way of living.

Introduction

| Day | 1 | Romans 1.1-15 | Paul's greetings, credentials, hopes |

Spiritual Bankruptcy of the World

Day	2	Romans 1.18-25	The wrath of God
	3	Romans 1.26-32	A great rebellion told by one who was a rebel
	4	Romans 2.1-11	All mankind condemned
	5	Romans 2.12-16	God's justice is always perfectly fair
	6	Romans 2.17-29	The true Israelite (a true Christian)
	7	Romans 3.1-8	Advantage and danger of privileges
	8	Romans 3.9-20	Terrible condemnation

New Way of Righteousness

Day	9	Romans 3.21-31	New hope for all
	10	Romans 4.1-12	Acceptance not dependent on circumcision
	11	Romans 4.13-25	Acceptance not dependent on law
	12	Romans 5.1-11	Rejoicing in the new life
	13	Romans 5.12-21	A stupendous contrast

Life on a New Level

Moral Effect of the New Way

A Living Church — Personal Messages

Stewardship

Our fourfold relationship to God carries implications (demands).

Relationship	Reason	Implication
Debtors	Because we have sinned	Repentance
Servants	Because he is Lord	Loving obedience
Sons	Because of his grace	Love
Stewards	Because all blessings come from God	Faithfulness

If I borrow money I can use it *as I please*; the only obligation is *to repay at the appointed time*. Here I am a *debtor*. A steward is not so. What he has is not borrowed for his use, but loaned him on trust, to be used as his master desires. His obligations are twofold:

1. He must use his master's gifts according to his master's will.

2. He has no obligation to repay but must give an account of his stewardship when his master asks for it.

This is what we mean by saying we are stewards of God's gifts. All that we are, all that we have, and all the latent possibilities within us are God's gifts, *to be used according to his will and for his glory*. Some day we must render an account of our stewardship.

Kinds of Stewards

A wise steward . . . whom the Lord finds doing his will (Luke 12.43).

A foolish steward . . . 'who knew his Lord's will, and prepared not himself, neither did according to his will' (Luke 12.47).

A slothful steward . . . who rationalized his laziness into a reproach against his Master; who distorted the facts into a reason for inaction (Matthew 25.24-30).

It is required in stewards, that a man be found faithful. (1 Corinthians 4.2)

Stewards of God's Gifts

Stewards of our bodies . . . to be kept fit and healthy; to be used wisely and unselfishly; to be kept clean, with its appetites under control. *How am I keeping my body?* (See Romans 12.1.)

Stewards of our minds . . . to be developed and trained; to be kept pure; to grow in wisdom and understanding until we have 'the mind that was in Christ'. *What am I doing with my mind?* (See Philippians 2.5.)

Stewards of our memories . . . to be stored with all that is beautiful, lofty, noble, and uplifting; to be used to comfort and strengthen, to encourage and uplift ourselves and others. *Is my memory being used in this way?* (See Philippians 4.8.)

Stewards of money, possessions, lands, education, gifts, and time . . . Do I look on these as God's or mine, to be used as I will or as he wills? Am I money's slave or is it my servant? Am I possessive with my possessions, or are they at the disposal of human need? What am I doing with the gift of education? Am I losing any of my talents through not using them? Time is precious; am I redeeming it? What do I do with my spare time? (See Luke 19.11-27.)

Stewards of an immortal soul . . . What does this mean? Some day my Lord will say, 'Give an account of thy stewardship.' (See Luke 16.2.)

THE HOLY SPIRIT

When you are converted and give your life to God, this is the work of the Holy Spirit. He comes and dwells in your heart (with you). That does not necessarily mean that you are filled by the Holy Spirit or have the fullness of the Spirit. There may be a dual control set up in your life, the Holy Spirit and you are in control. There may still be areas of your life that you will not allow the Holy Spirit to cleanse and control. *This dual control brings many conflicts* into your life which often find expression in anger, dissatisfaction and a critical spirit towards others.

The Fullness of the Spirit

In seeking the *fullness* of the Holy Spirit's power, it is often good to start with self-examination; that is, to place the moral standards before you and honestly face them. (See pages 28-9, 45-6.) Read them carefully; ponder over them prayerfully; apply them drastically.

We receive the fullness of the Holy Spirit by faith, just as we receive forgiveness. God offers; we, by faith, accept. 'If ye then, being evil, know how to give good gifts unto your children: how much more shall your heavenly Father give the Holy Spirit to them that ask him?' (Luke 11.13).

Remember the Holy Spirit is *holy*. His work in dwelling with us is to make us holy. He can never lead us to do things that are contrary to righteousness, love, or humility. His work is to make us like Jesus in character, outlook, attitudes and disposition. He changes our lives by dwelling with us, remaking the lost image. (See pages 44-5).

He never forces us to do his will, to go his way; but gently leads us. He leads us by the moral law, by the stirrings of conscience, by opening our eyes to new meaning in God's Word, by new responsibilities we realize we should carry, by inner convictions we know we should act on, and by many ways which we become more and more familiar with as we allow him to lead day by day.

The Holy Spirit gives us an outer witness that he is dwelling with us. This is apparent as the fruit of the Spirit. (See Galatians 5.22-23.)

1. *An obedient spirit.* 'Whoso keepeth his word, in him verily is the love of God perfected: hereby know we that we are in him' (1 John 2.5).

2. *Act righteously.* 'Every one that doeth righteousness is born of him' (1 John 2.29).

3. *Love God and love man.* 'Beloved, let us love one another . . . every one that loveth is born of God' (1 John 4.7).

He gives us an inner witness. This inner witness is accompanied by, and inseparable from, the outer witness.

1. *A conscience void of offence.*

2. *An inner assurance*, an inner conviction, an inner peace. I know whom I have believed. 'The Spirit itself beareth witness with our spirit, that we are the children of God' (Romans 8.16).

Led by the Spirit

There are always two ways of looking at any action. For example, going to the market. I might say, 'I went to the market.' That is the action seen from my point of view. Or I might say, 'I was led to the market by the need for food'. In one I went, in the other I was led. Both statements are correct and do not contradict each other. It is the same as regards being led by the Spirit.

I might say, 'I follow Jesus.'. . . . Here I am the actor. It is looking at it from my side, my determination, my will, my action.

I could say, 'I am led by the Spirit.' . . . Here I am the passive one. The Spirit is the Actor. I allow the Spirit to lead me. It is this allowing of one's life to be led by the Spirit that brings a greater sense of the presence of God in all the details of daily life. The great difference lies in that *in one my eyes are on myself, and in the other my eyes are on the Holy Spirit.*

Here is a practical method to try. As you rise in the morning ask God's Spirit to be with you during the day. You can be sure he will (this is faith), for God has promised his Spirit to all who ask (provided you are sincere and really mean what you say).

You may find that as the day goes on you become angry with someone. You think you had every right to be annoyed, but before long an inner conviction (the voice of the Holy Spirit, speaking in line with God's law, Matthew 5.21-26) suggests you should say you are sorry. *This is the Holy Spirit trying to lead you.* It isn't easy to follow, for pride says, 'Let it pass; it doesn't matter.' Which will you follow? You may let it pass, but God's Spirit does not leave you. Again during the day you may meet the person, and again the thought of saying you are sorry will pass through your mind. *This is God's Spirit trying once more to lead you.* You may still say no and allow pride to be your guide. God's Spirit will not leave you. At night, before going to sleep, you turn to pray. 'Thank you, Father, for the gift of thy Holy Spirit who has kept me and led me this day.' But as you say, 'led me', the thought may come to you again about the angry word and the way the Holy Spirit had tried to lead

111

you, but you would not be led. What are you going to do about it now? 'As many as are led by the Spirit of God, they are the sons of God' (Romans 8.14).

When you consistently refuse to obey God's Spirit in this way, your spiritual ear becomes dull, and before long the 'inner witness' of the Spirit becomes uncertain. You no longer speak of God's guidance as recent, personal and concrete, and soon the 'outer witness' becomes less noticeable and less challenging to the world.

Not only does God's Spirit lead us in this way, where he tries to keep us in right relationship with others by clearing all sin and inconsistencies out of our lives, but he also leads us into positive actions by bringing to our minds ways in which we can be helpful, duties we should perform, responsibilities we should undertake, etc.

> *I follow Jesus . . . Do I?*
> *I am led by the Spirit . . . Am I?*

Scripture Readings

While reading the passages, have constantly before you the questions, 'What has this to do with my life?' 'Am I filled with the Holy Spirit?' 'How can he become operative in my life?'

Prayer draws me close to God. *Self-surrender* gives God a chance to speak to me and work in me. *Faith* takes God at his word and accepts the gift offered. *Constant adjustment* of my life (ideas, attitudes, outlook, decisions) in loving obedience to the inner urge of God's Spirit, ensures his dwelling with me always.

The Holy Ghost — The Holy Spirit — The Comforter

Day			
	1	Ezekiel 37.1-14	New life through the Spirit
	2	Isaiah 11.1-9	The Spirit of God in man

Jesus and the Spirit

Day	3	Mark 1.1-11	Jesus—baptism of the Holy Spirit
	4	Luke 4.1-14	The Spirit in temptation
	5	Luke 4.14-22	The Spirit in Jesus' work
	6	John 3.1-17	Man's need of the Spirit

Promise of the Spirit

Day	7	John 14.15-26	Promised to those who obey (love)

Work of the Spirit

Day	8	John 15.26—16.3	To witness to Jesus
	9	John 16.1-11	To bring threefold conviction
	10	John 16.12-15	To bring spiritual illumination
	11	Acts 19.1-8	'Have ye received the Spirit?'
	12	Acts 1.1-9	Waiting for the Spirit
	13	Acts 2.1-13	Pentecost, the gift of the Spirit
	14	Luke 11.9-13	*Ask and appropriate the Spirit*

Characteristics of the Spirit

Day	15	Acts 2.22-40	1. Power
	16	Acts 4.1-12	2. Courage
	17	Acts 4.13-31	Courage
	18	Acts 6.1-15	3. Wisdom
	19	Acts 7.51-60	4. Unfaltering faith
	20	Acts 8.1-17	5. Evangelistic zeal
	21	Acts 10.1-18	6. Wider vision for world fellowship
	22	Acts 10.19-43	Wider vision for world fellowship
	23	Acts 10.44-48	Wider vision for world fellowship
	24	Acts 11.1-18	Wider vision for world fellowship
	25	Galatians 5.22-26	7. Character
	26	Galatians 6.1-10	8. Consideration, sympathy, humility
	27	Romans 8.1-17	9. Freedom, liberty

Home of the Spirit

Day	28	2 Corinthians 6.16-7.1	Our bodies—the temple of God's Spirit
	29	Philippians 2.1-15	Living in the Spirit

Final judgement is made on whether we have or have not his Spirit

They had his Spirit

Day 30 Matthew 25.31-40   Loving—they felt the sorrows of others

They hadn't his Spirit

Day 31 Matthew 25.41-46   Selfish—they did no great wrong as the world looks at wrong. Selfish, thoughtless, inconsiderate; they did not see; they did not feel; they did not help.

The 'Outer Witness' of God's Spirit

By their fruits ye shall know them. (Matthew 7.20)

The fruit of the Spirit is love, joy, peace, longsuffering, gentleness, goodness, faith, meekness, temperance. (Galatians 5.22-23)

This fruit does not come by 'trying to be good', it is the natural outcome of the Spirit dwelling in you. It is his love, his joy, his peace . . . expressing itself through your life. He brings willing obedience; he creates a hunger and thirst after righteousness; he inspires a love to God and man. The outward actions expressing this inward compulsion are the 'visible fruit' or 'outer witness' of God's Spirit. The 'outer' and 'inner' witness of the Spirit should always go hand in hand; if you have one without the other, something is wrong.

The inner witness by itself leads to an over-emphasis on the emotional side of religion. 'Why call ye me, Lord, Lord, and do not the things which I say?' (Luke 6.46).

The outer witness without the inner witness (assurance) is often due to religion being the following of standards, the observance of rules, a dependence on 'works', instead of a life of faith and fellowship.

114

The 'Inner Witness' of God's Spirit

A Conscience Void of Offence

As conscious beings we are capable of understanding the present and reflecting on the past.

> To remember, to bear witness to the present or the past is only one, and the least office of the conscience; its main business is to excuse or accuse, to approve or disapprove, to acquit or condemn. It is a faculty of power, implanted in every soul that comes into the world, of perceiving what is right or wrong in his own heart or life, in his tempers, thoughts, words and actions. (John Wesley)

The Christian rule of right and wrong is the Word of God. It is a light for his path and an instructor to educate his conscience. The Word of God is profitable
'for doctrine', to teach God's will;
'for reproof', to challenge all contrary to that will;
'for correction', to correct errors in basic thinking;
'for instruction', to train the conscience to lead us in the paths of righteousness (2 Timothy 3.16).
When this enlightened conscience brings no accusation, disapproval or condemnation, it is a conscience void of offence.

An Inner Assurance

The presence of the Spirit brings an inner conviction, an inner peace. How do I know I love God with a humble joy, and find delight in his presence, and rejoice in loving obedience? How do I know I love a person and find delight in his company? There are the outward acts that testify to it; there is the inner testimony that I alone have. So is it with God. 'The Spirit itself beareth witness with our spirit, that we are the children of God' (Romans 8.16). *Every Christian should have the inner and outer witness of God's Spirit.*

VICTORY

Victory over Temptation

The temptations that come to people vary widely in their nature, and no one is free from them. Some temptations come so suddenly and with such force that it appears to us impossible to overcome them.

Victory comes by a practical confidence in God and acting on the promises he has given us.

Some temptations can be faced in prayer long before they come. In your Quiet Time as you think of the coming day, you may realize that a situation will arise that day bringing a concrete temptation. Face it before it comes. Claim God's power then and there, so that when the situation arises your mind will go back to the morning prayer and you will find it easier to act along the lines that God has dictated to you through your conscience. You are forearmed by having already faced the temptation.

The power in many temptations lies in the defeatist attitude in which we face them. God expects us to overcome, and we shall overcome only when we approach them with faith—faith in God's power, confident that in God's strength we shall be conquerors. 'God . . . will not suffer you to be tempted above that ye are able' is a promise we can depend on at all times (1 Corinthians 10.13).

Keep your eyes off yourself and on your Saviour.

Keep your eyes off your weakness and on God's strength. 'My grace is sufficient for thee: for my strength is made perfect in weakness' (2 Corinthians 12.9). We can rely on his strength. Jesus faced his temptations in the wilderness by bringing his mind to think of the foundations on which his life was built: *God first. Trust him absolutely.*

Victory over Fear

Fear paralyzes all our powers. We fail because we fear. If you feel afraid, stop and quietly in God's presence, ask yourself why. Be honest in giving the reason. Do not let your feeling of fear dictate your action. When convinced something should be done, go ahead and do it despite the feeling of fear. God's power is at your disposal. Paul said, 'I can do all things [all things God wants me to do] through Christ which strengtheneth me' (Philippians 4.13). He had learned to appropriate the strength and power God had put at his disposal.

When a decision is made, do not be anxious or doubtful as to the result. *Trust absolutely*: remember, God asks faithfulness; the rest can be left in his hands.

Each person has his own fears. Common ones are: fear of what others will think or say; fear of making restitution; fear of apologizing, due to the loss of face it brings; fear of being different from others; timidity, or distrust of oneself; fear of the future, etc.

Fear comes by looking at oneself or others instead of looking at Jesus. Jesus said, 'Be not afraid [of what the crowd thinks or does], only believe' (Mark 5.36).

To believe means to act on what in your heart you know is right. Faith acts—victory follows.

Are you afraid in any situation? Stop a moment, surrender the feeling to God, *make a decision which fully satisfies your conscience*, and act quietly but firmly on it. This act is faith, the faith that overcomes the world of fear. God in this way will teach you to overcome all kinds of fear. *He can do this only with your trustful co-operation.*

Victory over Death

Jesus Christ . . . hath abolished death, and hath brought life and immortality to light through the gospel. 2 Timothy 1.10

O death, where is thy sting? O grave, where is thy victory? The sting of death is sin; and the strength of sin is the law. But thanks be to God, which giveth us the victory through our Lord Jesus Christ. (1 Corinthians 15.55-57)

The secret of victory over death, and the assurance of immortality, is not an argument of the mind, it is the conviction of the heart. It is reached through faith, by those who trust Christ and experience the love of God by committing their lives to him, accepting his promises, his challenges, and his rebukes. This life brings its own assurance. It stirs the conviction that in the love of God revealed in Jesus and in the communion and fellowship we have with him here and now, we have something that is eternal.

'Thanks be to God, who giveth us the victory.'

A Prayer for a Victorious Attitude at All Times

Father, I pray that no circumstances, however bitter or however long drawn out, may cause me to break thy law, the law of love to thee and to my neighbour. That I may not become resentful, have hurt feelings, hate, or become embittered by life's experiences, but that in and through all, I may see thy guiding hand and have a heart full of gratitude for thy daily mercy, daily love, daily power and daily presence.

Help me in the day when I need it most to remember that:

All things work together for good to them that love God. (Romans 8.28)

I can do all things through Christ which strengthen me. (Philippians 4.13)

[God said], My grace is sufficient for thee: for my strength is made perfect in thy weakness. (2 Corinthians 12.9)

Scripture Readings

These readings are short ones. Read them over. Spend a few minutes asking yourself what they mean for you today, under your circumstances. 'When thou passest through the waters [the wide, wide waters that demand perseverance; the unseen, unsailed waters that demand faith and confidence; the cruel pitiless waters that demand patience, courage, and unfailing love[, *I will be with thee*' (Isaiah 43.2, italics added).

Victory — By Dependence on God's Strength

Day		
1	Matthew 4.1-13	By the right use of the Bible
2	Mark 14.32-42	By having a dominant purpose
3	Mark 14.66-72	Forfeited through fear
4	Acts 4.5-22	By making conscience the dictator of action
5	Acts 4.23-31	By the joy of pleasing God
6	Acts 5.17-32	By obedience
7	Romans 7.15-25	Lost by being led by natural desires
8	Romans 8.1-11	By being led by the Spirit
9	Romans 8.31-39	Through the Ever Victorious
10	2 Corinthians 2.7-10	By confidence in the adequacy of God's grace
11	Galatians 5.15-26	By crucifixion

12	Ephesians 6.10-18	By being fully equipped
13	Philippians 4.10-13	Because of adequate resources
14	2 Timothy 4.14-18	By being on God's side
15	Genesis 45.1-15	By magnanimity
16	Romans 12.9-21	By a counter offensive of love
17	Hebrews 11.23-27	By faith (seeing the invisible)
18	Hebrews 11.32—12.3	By faith (right values, first things first)

Comforted (Strengthened) in Times of Hardship and Suffering

Comfort means to be strengthened by having God (a friend) *with you.*

Day	19	Joshua 1.1-9	Strengthened to face new responsibilities
	20	Acts 12.1-12	Prayer changes things
	21	Matthew 11.25-30	Strengthened by sharing our yoke
	22	Romans 9.18-30	Strengthened by right comparisons
	23	2 Corinthians 1.3-11	Strengthened to strengthen others
	24	2 Corinthians 4.8-18	Knocked down but *never* knocked out
	25	2 Corinthians 12.7-10	Man's weakness is God's opportunity
	26	2 Timothy 4.1-8	Hard times coming; strengthened by hope and example
	27	Hebrews 13.3-13	Strengthened by the unvarying dependability of God
	28	1 Peter 1.3-9	Strengthened by regarding temptation as testing
	29	1 Peter 5.6-11	Strengthened by a humble attitude, a carefree mind, a vigilant spirit

The Fully Surrendered Life Is the Fully Victorious Life

Day	30	Psalm 16.1-11	The surrendered life is the happy life

Victory over Circumstances

When thou passest through the waters, I will be with thee. (Isaiah 43.2)

God does not say that because you believe in him, he will keep you from hardship and suffering. He says, if you trust him, he will strengthen you to meet all the experiences of life in a conquering spirit. You will have secret resources of power to call on when they are needed.

Life is full of hard experiences, bitter disappointments, unexpected losses, grim tragedies. How do Christians face these? Here are several thoughts that may be of help.

1. Evil does not come from God but comes through the sin, malice, callousness, passions, selfishness, and neglect of man. *God is not responsible for these.*

There are also disasters, calamities and accidents which are the other side of the privilege and joy of living in such a world as this. If there were no spice of risk, there would be no zest of adventure.

2. Sometimes evil comes through the direct malice of man. It is easy to harbour feelings of hate, a desire to be God's instrument of vengeance. It is a terrible thing to fall into the hands of a hate like that. For hate desolates both the wronged and the wrongdoer. *This work of punishment is not ours but God's.*

It is a perilous position for any man to take up that he is the instrument of the judgement of God. God is working in the hearts of those who have wronged us as well as in our hearts. His mills are grinding out resistlessly the judgements of righteousness. Leave all to God. The justice of God is far more sure and unerring, for it is the justice of love, a love that will not let men go, but follows them still through all the mazes of their flight from it, till it brings them to redemption. *It is this vision of God behind the scenes that calms the heart and takes away the restless heat of rancour and revenge*. It is this that helps one to face all in a magnanimous spirit.

3. Circumstances may appear to wreck our lives and God's plans, but *God is not helpless among the ruins*. Our broken lives are not lost or useless. God's love is still working. He comes in and takes the calamity and uses it victoriously, working out his wonderful plan of love. 'All things work together for good to them that love God.' He is always master of the situation. There is infinite resourcefulness in the almighty love. Many a man has become great in spite of, as well as because of, disaster. This is the victory of God's love, but it does not come to all. It comes to those who keep their faith clear, and their lives clean towards God. It comes to those who keep in touch with the divine love, are linked to the divine will, and look for chances of helping on the purposes they are sure God still has for them. 'This is the victory that overcomes the world, [the world of disaster] even our faith.'

[Thoughts based on *The Victory of God* by James Reid.]

THE FELLOWSHIP—THE CHURCH

The church is not just an organization. When we speak of the church we very often have in mind some building, our own local congregation and its familiar activities, or the organization behind it. These are not the Church; they are the scaffolding necessary because of the limitations of our common human nature.

Christ founded a fellowship: the Church.

The Head of the Church

The Church owns no other king than Christ and claims the freedom to obey his will in all things. People have braved the anger of kings and willingly endured persecution and martyrdom rather than be disloyal to the commands of their divine Lord.

The Church—Holiness, Fellowship, Unity

The character, outlook, motives, attitudes of Jesus, the head of the Church, can be summed up in one word—*holy*. It includes all that is beautiful and pleasing to God. What he was like, he expected the Church to be like. 'Christ loved the church and gave himself for it; . . . that he might present it to himself a glorious church, not having spot, or wrinkle, or any such thing; but that it should be holy and without blemish' (Ephesians 5.25, 27).

Jesus gathered around him a scattered band of people

123

held together by the invisible bonds of fellowship. It was this sense of fellowship and the need for it that first drew close the bonds of union among Christians and brought about the organization of the Church.

The Church is a fellowship of those who believe in God, are reconciled to him through Christ and are made one in Christ. It openly professes that faith and comes together in a corporate life and activity on that basis.

The Church is a fellowship of those who strive to live according to the law of love which Christ taught by word and example. It undertakes to regulate its own life by that law and to make it effective in the life of the world by every means in its power. Hence, membership in the organized church involves a personal vow of obedience to Christ's law of love and a confession of faith in God through Christ.

Live Righteously—Radiate Love

The natural outcome of faith and love should be unity. Christ means his disciples to be knit together in a single fellowship as harmonious as the unity of a healthy body. But alas! The organized Church is desperately ill. There is plenty of room for different types of services, methods of organization, and differences of opinion. It is not the will of Christ that there should be bitter rivalry and ill will among the different organizations. This is contrary to his Spirit; it is breaking his Body, which is the Church.

It is not uniformity but unity that is part of the essential nature of the fellowship (Church).

Beware of bigotry and spiritual pride. 'We saw one casting out devils in thy name; and we forbad him, because he followeth not with us' (Luke 9.49).

Beware of prejudice and narrow-mindedness. Let truth and love, justice and mercy mingle so that the Spirit of truth and love may lead you.

124

Beware of a broadmindedness that has no solid foundation for its opinions and outlook.

A guiding attitude:

> In things essential—unity
> In things doubtful—liberty
> In all things—charity

The Church—Worship, Witness, Work

Worship is the natural expression of Christian faith. Wherever men and women have been led by Christ into faith and love towards the Father, they have been impelled to come together to express that faith and love in common acts of praise and prayer. The organized Church should help to make that worship spontaneous and sincere.

Jesus came to proclaim the kingdom of God, to offer its blessings to those who would take heed, and to instruct people in its obligations and responsibilities. When he left he committed to the Church the duty of carrying on this work. The Church is his voice in the world announcing the good news about God, calling men everywhere to repent, and inviting them to enter the kingdom. *Every individual in the Church shares this responsibility*. We are called to witness. Are we doing it?

Jesus went about doing good. The Church should do the same for it is called to an active ministry of loving service. Social reform, just and better conditions, righting wrongs, lightening people's burdens—these are all part of the work of the Church, and in it *every individual has his part to play*. What am I doing? Am I a spectator or am I an active worker? Is God likely to say to me, 'Well done, thou good and faithful servant: . . . enter thou into the joy of thy Lord' (Matthew 25.21)?

Scripture Readings

Keep the subjects of fellowship and unity before you throughout the month. Ponder over the basis on which they can be made a reality. What breaks them? Am I prepared to discard those elements in me? What makes them? Am I prepared to cultivate those elements in me? If I am not prepared to do these two things, the dream of fellowship and unity will remain a dream. Do I really want it with all my heart?

> The sin I impute to each frustrate ghost
> Is—the unlit lamp and the ungirt loin.
>> Robert Browning

The Fellowship—The Church

Day			
	1	Matthew 16.13-20	On this rock I build my Church
	2	Acts 2.1-4; 14-21	The Church's endowment
	3	Ephesians 1.15-23	The head of the Church
	4	Ephesians 5.25-33	Christ's love for the Church
	5	Ephesians 3.14-21	Rooted in faith and love
	6	Galatians 6.1-10	The attitudes of fellowship
	7	Ephesians 4.1-6	The outlook necessary for unity
	8	1 Corinthians 12.1-11	The outlook necessary for unity
	9	1 Corinthians 12.12-14	The outlook necessary for unity
	10	1 Corinthians 12.15-20	The outlook necessary for unity
	11	1 Corinthians 12.21-26	The outlook necessary for unity
	12	1 Corinthians 12.27-31	The outlook necessary for unity
	13	Revelation 7.9-17	The Church triumphant
	14	Psalm 34.1-22	The solid life of reverence (fear)
	15	Psalm 112.1-10	The solid life of righteousness
	16	Psalm 125.1-5	The solid life of trust

The Christmas Story

Day			
	17	Isaiah 9.1-7	The coming Prince
	18	Isaiah 11.1-10	The coming King

The Christmas Story — The Christmas Spirit

At Christmas we celebrate the birth of Jesus. It was the day when God gave his greatest gift, his Son, to mankind.

A Time of Joy

Joy, because of all he has meant to the world, and still means to everyone who allows him into their hearts. Because the news of the birth of Jesus is joyous to us, we try to radiate that joy to others.

> Joy to the world! the Lord is come:
>   Let earth receive her King;
> Let every heart prepare him room,
>   And heaven and nature sing.
>
> Isaac Watts

A Time for Unselfish Giving

As God gave us his greatest gift this day, so we have learned to give gifts to one another or to send some message of cheer.

A Time for being Thoughtful for Others

We think of those less fortunate than ourselves. The world is full of people who have heavy burdens to carry—the poor who struggle in their poverty, the sick who fight an uphill battle against disease; the maimed who have been so handicapped, the blind whose lot we can never fully understand, the orphans deprived of many of the priceless privileges we have, and countless others. This is the time when we can share with them some of the material benefits God has given to us.

A Time for being Generous

Generous with our money, generous in our speech, generous in our help, generous to all.

When we live through Christmas like this, there is a great joy and happiness in our hearts. It is only natural, for joy and happiness are by-products of generosity, kindness, mercy, sympathy and love. This is the spirit in which Jesus lived. It is the spirit in which he meant all his followers to live, not just at Christmas time, but throughout the whole year.

Will you allow Jesus to become ruler of your life this Christmas, that the spirit of Christmas may dwell in your heart? The spirit of Christmas is generous in outlook, kind in disposition, thoughtful for others, sensitive to suffering, unselfish in giving. Happy are those who have this spirit.

The Close of the Year

Thanks and Praise

Look back over the past year, counting your blessings, remembering God's goodness and mercy in a spirit of thankfulness and praise. 'Praise God from whom all blessings flow.'

Dedication and Surrender

After praising and thanking God for all his goodness and mercy, dedicate or rededicate your life to God for his use in the coming year. 'I beseech you therefore, brethren, by the mercies of God, that ye present your bodies a living sacrifice, holy, acceptable unto God, which is your reasonable service' (Romans 12.1).

PART 3

The Disciple and the Church

HELPS FOR NEW CHRISTIANS

You are joining the Church, you are becoming part of the Church Universal. *It is a priceless privilege—it carries with it great responsibilities.* Here are a few thoughts to help you in the Christian life.

1. *Never neglect your prayers morning and evening.* Prayer is like breathing. Stop breathing and you die; stop praying and your Christian experience will soon fade away.

2. *Read some verses of Scripture every day*, and ask God to help you take from them something that will enable you to live that day's life well. Bible study is like taking food; it nourishes the spiritual life.

3. Remember that by a beautiful character, kind actions and a right attitude to life you are witnessing all the time for Christ. Learn to witness vocally too. *Witnessing is like taking exercise; it makes you strong.*

4. *Be regular in your attendance at the Sunday services.* Be a member of some class for systematic Bible study. Give as liberally as you can to the support of the church.

5. Seek some definite work in connection with your church. Do it with all your might. Let 'Every church member a worker' be your motto.

6. Keep in mind the glorious history of the Church, cherish the things for which it stands, and do your best to be found a worthy member of it. Do not try to defend the un-Christlike things the Church has sometimes done in the past, but be ready to own that they were wrong. Learn from these mistakes. You cannot justify an un-Christlike action.

7. Be honest—truthful—loving—unselfish. Watch and pray

against all impurity in thought, in mind, and in deed. Be alert to help others and in every way prove yourself to be a loyal servant of the Lord Jesus Christ.

8. *Make a friend of your minister.* Honour him for his office as a servant of God. Give him all the sympathy and help you can. Go to him in trouble and perplexity, to seek comfort and counsel.

BAPTISM

The Symbol

In our ordinary lives we use water for washing off the dust and dirt of the world. In the sacrament of baptism water is the 'element' used to convey to us the spiritual cleansing which is necessary before anyone can enter into the new life which God is willing to give us.

The Scriptural Authority
for the Sacrament of Baptism

In Matthew 28.19, our Lord definitely commissions his apostles to 'make disciples of all the nations, baptizing them into the name of the Father and of the Son and of the Holy Ghost' (RV). These words are called the Institution of the Sacrament.

In obedience to the teaching so given, we find that the apostles accompanied their first preaching of Christ with the administration of baptism, and in the story of the primitive Church, as told in the Acts of the Apostles, baptism is universally accepted as the method by which people were admitted into the membership of the Church.

In the Epistles of the New Testament baptism is regarded as the sacrament by which men entered into the 'new' life which Paul describes as 'in Christ'. Further, the moral teaching contained in the Epistles rests on the ground of baptism. Wrongdoing was worthy of rebuke at all times, but wrongdoing on the part of those who had been baptized into Jesus Christ became more serious, because it contradicted and perverted the 'new' nature which they had received from God, of which baptism had been the sign and seal.

Scripture Readings—Baptism of Adults

Acts 2.37-42	First preaching and the first baptisms
Acts 8.35-40; 10.44-48	Baptisms by Philip and Peter
Acts 16.25-34	Baptism by Paul
Romans 6.1-11	Baptism as burial and resurrection
Colossians 2.8-15	Baptism as a putting on of Christ
Galatians 3.27	Baptism as a putting on of Christ
Mark 1.1-8	The baptism by John the Baptist
Matthew 28.18-20	The Christian institution
Mark 16.15-16	The Christian institution

The Meaning of Baptism

When John the Baptist came to prepare the way of the Lord, he came 'preaching the baptism of repentance unto the remission of sins'. John demanded a moral purification. He baptized people in order to give some outward expression to their inward and spiritual change. By the symbol of water he assured his converts of their cleansing, the stains of the old life being washed away.

Yet whatever blessing this rite conveyed, John knew that his baptism was only preparatory. 'I indeed baptize you with water; but one mightier than I cometh, . . . he shall baptize you with the Holy Ghost and with fire' (Luke 3.16).

Fire is the symbol of enthusiasm, *and to be baptized with the Holy Ghost means not only to be cleansed from evil, but to be fired with a new enthusiasm for righteousness.*

Baptized 'Into the Name'

The apostles are told to baptize 'in' or 'into the name of the Father, and of the Son, and of the Holy Ghost'. These words, *into the Name*, are of great significance. In the Scriptures the 'Name' of God stands for all whereby he makes himself known. *To be baptized 'into the Name' symbolizes not only the break with the past life, but the entering into a new life revealed in Jesus Christ and made possible for us through the fellowship of the Holy Spirit.*

Christian baptism thus becomes not only the representation of the spiritual cleansing that God gives to man in Jesus Christ, but also the means by which that blessing is conveyed to man in response to his profession of faith. When baptism is administered something vital happens. The baptized person not only receives the confirmation of his new life, but the new privileges, and the new fellowship which he now shares, give him strength to face the new duties and responsibilities of the Christian life.

The sacrament of baptism admits us into a fellowship in which, if we incur new responsibilities, we also share all the privileges of God's children.

[Thoughts based on *Christian Faith and Practice* and used by permission]

For the dedication and/or baptism of infants, see the Appendix.

THE COMMUNION OF THE LORD'S SUPPER

The New Covenant—The New Testament

God's Side

When Jesus instituted the sacrament of the Lord's Supper, he took the cup and said, 'This cup is the new testament [covenant] in my blood' (Luke 22.20). The cup is the sign of the new relationship into which God, through the reconciling work of Christ, enters with people.

God had said to Israel, 'I will be your God and ye shall be my people.' That was the *Old Covenant* (Testament) by which God chose this nation, and the Passover Feast was its memorial.

In Jesus Christ we have a *New Covenant* (Testament) which God has made with those who accept Jesus Christ as their Lord and Saviour, and of that new relationship the Lord's Supper is the sign and seal. In it we have the assurance from God of:

a. all that we need for our Christian life;
b. the forgiveness of sins;
c. his presence with us to enable us to overcome the world.

All this is promised as God's side of the New Covenant.

Man's Side

The word *sacrament* is taken from the military life of Rome. The *sacramentum* was the oath the Roman soldier took that he would be loyal to the emperor and serve the country with his life. *That is the pledge we give at the Communion table.* Christ is Lord of our lives and as such we undertake:

a. to consecrate ourselves (our minds, our hearts, our wills) to Christ's service;

b. To follow where he leads.

This is man's pledge in the New Covenant.

Historical Background

The Jews had kept the Feast of the Passover year by year, ever since God, by the hand of Moses, had set them free from the bondage of Egypt. (See Exodus 12.)

It was at the Feast of the Passover that Jesus inaugurated the Lord's Supper. (See Luke 22.1-23.)

Knowing human nature as he did, our Lord not only appointed a special time when his disciples should 'remember him' in thought and meditation; he gave them something to 'do'. Knowing what the observance of the Passover had meant for generation after generation of the Jewish people, he instituted a new Feast which would forever be intimately connected with his death in everything that was associated with it.

The Lord's Supper as a Memorial

In Memory of Him

'This do in remembrance of me.' We come to the Lord's table to call to remembrance his life and death, to recall his teaching and to give thanks for his example. All this we do, and more. We come to meet him there. To come to the sacrament of the Lord's Supper is just like a person going to jesus while he was on earth. *To those who went without any intention of obedience, he could not reveal himself.* To those who went with a real difficulty, he gave light; to the penitent, he gave his gospel of forgiveness; to the weak, he gave new strength and character; to the sorrowful, he gave comfort.

We meet our Lord here; it is with him we keep this holy tryst. The bread and wine speak to us of him. 'This is *my body*.' 'This cup is the new testament in *my blood*.'

Of this deep truth of the presence of the living Christ with and in his people the sacrament is the sign and seal. It was given to the disciples not so much to bring to them the words and example of their Master, great though these are, but to bring his own person. Bread and wine are the outward symbols of his invisible presence.

In Memory of His Death

'My blood . . . shed . . . for the remission of sins' (Matthew 26.28). These words that Jesus used when instituting this Feast make it quite clear that he was thinking of his death as the sacrifice he was about to make for the sins of the world.

The likeness that exists between the Jewish Passover (see Exodus 12) and the Christian sacrament is most striking, and there is no doubt that it is against this background that we have to read what Jesus said and did.

The Passover	*The Sacrament*
A lamb	Jesus, the Lamb of God (John 1.29)
A lamb slain . . . flesh eaten . . . blood used	Bread, 'my body'; wine, 'my blood' to show forth his death'
A memorial of deliverance from bondage to Egypt	A memorial of deliverance from the bondage of sin

However much there is that is mysterious and difficult about these thoughts, they say one thing very clearly to each one of us: 'Christ died—for me.' The sacrament brings to us the message of the cross. When we look at the cross of Jesus Christ, we begin to understand what it cost God to forgive the sin of the world. Sin is not a thing that can be cancelled by a stroke of the pen. Sin can only be conquered by the power of sacrifice. The cross is God conquering sin by sacrifice, in order that he might redeem man from the bondage of sin and set us free to live for and with him.

When we break the bread and when we pour out the wine, we hold up the symbols that give expression to that one perfect sacrifice, and we pray the Father who gave his Son on our behalf to accept us. God can accept us only if we truly consecrate ourselves to him. *That is where there is sacrifice in the Sacrament—we identify ourselves with Christ's sacrifice.* It is a sacrifice of the spirit. To forgive the person who has wronged us, to love our enemy, to conquer pride, to deny the sins that do so easily beset us, to deny ourselves and take up our cross—these all mean sacrifice. And unless we make the sacrifice, the cross that Jesus bore for us has not brought us into reconciliation with God.

The Lord's Supper as Communion

Communion with Christ—
His Presence, Nourishment, Growth

The sacrament as a communion says to us that as the Lord Jesus was physically present with his disciples in the Upper Room, so we can enter into fellowship with his spiritual presence here and now. This is where in a simple sense he has promised to be with us. It is by appointment that we meet him at his table.

Jesus said, 'My meat is to do the will of him that sent me' (John 4.34). He found that in obedience he could fully realize the joy of fellowship with the Father. In the same way, as we accept and apply Jesus' teaching, we find an enriched fellowship with him which nourishes our souls, that is, develops our understanding, sympathy, humility and love. In this fellowship we find power to live a higher life, a life that overcomes the world. He nourishes us.

Jesus said, 'I am the vine, ye are the branches . . . without me ye can do nothing' (John 15.5). Only as we receive Jesus Christ, and as he enters into us, are we able to live the Christian life. It is our fellowship with him that helps us to conquer our bad temper, irritability, pride, and resentment, as well as to reject the grosser temptations of life. It is our fellowship with him that helps us to act towards one another in a spirit of love. Many have found the act of Communion the means of grace by which they are best able to realize this great truth of abiding in Christ, and Christ in us.

Communion with Fellow Christians

The sacrament also has its social aspect. From the beginning the disciples used to meet together for a service in memory of our Lord, which they called the Breaking of Bread. At first it was an ordinary meal (called the Love Feast) and ended with the Lord's Supper being observed. In this way it was a reminder that Christian discipleship is not a solitary life, but a life in which we are united together in a great fellowship because of our common relationship to Jesus Christ. Our fellowship with Christ finds expression in a spirit of brotherhood in our attitudes to, and conduct with, one another.

Communion with the Saints

The fellowship of those we have known and loved is never more real than when we join with others in the act of Communion with our Lord and Saviour. We are part of, and in fellowship with, those who have gone before, who by faith subdued kingdoms, wrought righteousness, lived

142

lovingly; who by patiently enduring, suffering, and serving have worked for his kingdom on earth.

The Lord's Supper as Thanksgiving (Eucharist)

Sometimes the Lord's Supper is called the *Eucharist*, from a Greek word which means 'thanksgiving'. In instituting this memorial of himself, Jesus looked beyond the dark shadow of death that was around him and gave to the Feast the character of 'thanksgiving'. As such it was observed by his apostles after our Lord's resurrection had restored their faith. They became men who rejoiced that they were counted worthy to suffer for the Name (Acts 5.41), and their holy joy in the service of their Master found its highest expression in the observance of his memorial. This sacrament has always been the great act of the Church's thanksgiving, in which adoration, gratitude, joy and love all have their part. However solemn the act is, we should be filled not with sadness but with holy joy. We are giving thanks to God for his gift of 'new life in Jesus Christ'. Communion with Christ must be a Eucharist.

When we remember Christ's love for us—all he has done for us, all he is to us, and all he is able to do for us—we learn to rejoice in observing the Sacrament that draws us into closer union with him.

Preparation for Coming to the Lord's Supper

The promise that we give in the Sacrament of the Lord's Supper is of such a solemn and exacting nature that no one of us has any right at any time to go to the Lord's table unless he realizes what God is offering him, and what he is promising God. (See page 138, man's side of the New Covenant.) Let us examine ourselves as regards our discipleship.

1. Are we willing, for Christ's sake, to give up everything we know to be wrong?

2. To do some difficult duty we feel we should do?

3. To put right relationships that are not in accordance with God's law or God's will?

4. To deny ourselves, take up our cross daily, and follow him?

These are some of the questions we must face if there is to be any spiritual union of our life with his risen life.

God asks 'willingness' to obey, not 'worthiness' of life, for no one is worthy. We come to his table in our need.

Face the sacredness of your vow. 'Let a man examine himself, and so let him eat of that bread, and drink of that cup' (1 Corinthians 11.28).

[Thoughts based on *Christian Faith and Practice* and used by permission.]

Scripture Readings

The Sacrament as a Memorial

Exodus 12.1-28	The Passover—historical background
Jeremiah 31.31-34	The promise of the New Covenant
Isaiah 53.1-12	The Suffering Servant
Luke 22.1-13	The preparation for the Feast
Luke 22.14-20	The Holy Supper instituted
1 Corinthians 11.23-24	The Holy Communion

The Sacrament as Communion

John 14.15-24	The fellowship of the Spirit
Revelation 3.20	'I will sup with thee'
Ephesians 3.14-19	Communion with Christ; his presence
Galatians 2.20	Communion with Christ; his presence
John 6.32-51	Communion with Christ; his nourishment
John 15.1-11	Communion with Christ; his growth
Hebrews 12.1-2	The communion of saints
Revelation 7.9-17	The communion of saints

The Sacrament as Thanksgiving and Pledge

Matthew 22.1-14	The wedding garment
Psalm 139.1-24	Self-examination
Psalm 51.1-19	Confession
Isaiah 55.1-13	Invitation
John 15.1-11	Obligation—communion with Christ
John 13.1-15	Obligation—humble service to man

THE THREE GREAT FESTIVALS
OF THE CHURCH

Christmas

For the readings connected with Christmas and the thoughts connected with it, see pages 127-9. At Christmas we celebrate the birth of Jesus Christ.

Easter

At Easter we remember the death and resurrection of our Lord Jesus Christ. The Church has always laid a great emphasis on this season of the year. There would have been no Church had there been no Easter. The Church has its foundations deep in historical facts. By the vote of the people, Pilate crucified Jesus. He was put to death on what is now called Good Friday. Everyone thought that to be the end. If it had been the end, then Jesus would only have been one more of the murdered prophets; there would have been no Christian Church. But the cross was not the last word—it was the prelude to Easter.

The Christian Church rests on the assurance that Jesus rose from the dead and is a living and active person, working in human life here and now.

This is the central and dominating fact of the Christian gospel. 'Because I live, ye shall live also.' Not because he lived, but because he is living *now*, do they have life.

Had there been no resurrection, the first disciples would never have preached Christ at all.

As Easter approaches, Christians remember the suffering these days brought to their Lord, so many make it a time of special self-denials in order that they might enter more fully into 'the fellowship of his suffering'.

Easter Sunday comes as a day of rejoicing. The night of sorrow has passed; the day of joy has come. He is not dead, but living. Hallelujah! Because of this fact—the resurrection of Jesus Christ—Easter has become one of the great festivals of the Christian Church.

Pentecost

At Whitsuntide (the feast of Pentecost) we celebrate the coming of the Holy Spirit in power to the first disciples, who had followed Jesus during his lifetime. The resurrection was not enough to make the disciples equal to the tremendous task of carrying the gospel to the whole world. Something else was needed. They were told to wait at Jerusalem for the baptism of the Holy Spirit. 'Ye shall receive power, after that the Holy Ghost is come upon you: and ye shall be witnesses unto me . . . unto the uttermost part of the earth' (Acts 1.8).

They waited in fellowship and prayer, and seven weeks after that first Easter morning, the promise was fulfilled— the Holy Spirit came upon them. (Read Acts 2.) The day was called Pentecost, the Hebrew harvest festival. This was the signal for the Church to arise and, under the leadership of the Holy Spirit, to launch into action. This was the equipment they needed. The Holy Spirit brought into their lives new insight, new power, new courage, new initiative, new discipline, and new leadership.

Festival	Historical Fact	Emphasis	Thanksgiving for
Christmas	Birth of Jesus	'God with us'	'His unspeakable gift'
Passion Week	Death of Jesus (the cross)	'The fellowship of his suffering'	'By his stripes we are healed'
Easter	Resurrection	Rejoice! New life!	'The power of his resurrection'
Pentecost	The coming of the Holy Spirit	Power, enthusiasm, liberty	'The fruit of the Spirit'

Scripture Readings

Readings for Christmas

See pages 126-7. Christmas is a fixed date, December 25.

Readings for the Easter Season

The date for Easter varies from the end of March to the end of April. The readings that follow are taken from *Morning Prayers and Readings for School and Family*, arranged by Mrs Guy Rogers.

The Beginning of the Passion Story
Mark 11.1-10	The entry into Jerusalem
Luke 20.9-18	The unthankful husbandmen
Luke 20.19-26	The tribute to Caesar
Matthew 23.1-12	The Pharisees
Mark 14.3-9	The alabaster box
Matthew 26.17-30	The Last Supper

The Events Leading to the Cross
John 13.1-17	The washing of the disciples' feet
Luke 22.31-38	Peter's oath
Mark 14.32-50	The garden of Gethsemane

Luke 22.54-62	Peter's denial
Luke 22.66-71	The trial by Caiaphas
Luke 23.1-12	Pilate and Herod

Passion Week, the Last Week of Jesus' Life

Matthew 27.11-26	Pilate's decision
Matthew 27.27-37	The mocking
John 19.17-30	The crucifixion
1 Corinthians 11.23-29	The institution of the Lord's Supper
Luke 23.32-46	The crucifixion; *Good Friday*

Eastertide, 'Christ is Risen!'

John 20.1-10	Easter Sunday
John 20.11-18	The appearance to Mary Magdalene
John 20.19-31	The appearance to Thomas
John 21.1-14	The appearance on the seashore
John 21.15-19	The forgiveness of Peter
Luke 24.44-53	The Ascension

Other readings can be found on page 60, March 12 to March 31. Read also pages 56-8.

Readings for Pentecost

See the readings for October, especially from the 7th to the 20th. Read also the whole section on pages 109-15.

Appendix

INFANT BAPTISM OR DEDICATION

The question of infant baptism or dedication arises only when there are Christian parents. As soon as the Christian society became established, infant baptism became the practice of the Church. The unity of the family is one of the underlying truths of life. Infant baptism gives expression to this fact.

The practice of infant baptism rests also upon the revelation of God given us in Jesus Christ. That revelation makes clear to us that, *in the matter of our salvation, God always acts first.* God does not wait for man's repentance; he sends his Son to bring about that repentance. He comes to meet us, and our experience of his love creates the spirit of new obedience. *Everywhere and always it is God who takes the initiative.* The administration of the sacrament of baptism to infants gives a symbolic expression to that primary note in the Christian gospel and is true to the mind of God.

It is in line with this thought that the beautiful incident of our Lord blessing the little children finds its place (Mark 10.13). That is not a warrant for infant baptism, but it emphatically shows that our Lord's blessing was not confined to those who came to him in conscious love or penitence. Further, the words 'for of such is the kingdom of heaven' imply the present membership of the little ones in the heavenly Father's family.

If a child dies before it is baptized, it does not mean that it is damned. God is not like that.

Baptism of the child expresses in symbolic form our trust that God's Spirit will take the initiative in seeking to dwell with and work in and through that child's life.

Baptism is also an act of dedication on the part of the parents. They recognize that the child is a gift from God and they dedicate him or her to God's service, promising to do all they can to lead the child to know, love and follow God.

FOR FURTHER READING

The following books are listed under the topics discussed in each chapter. The starred titles are those recommended by Eric Liddell. In all cases the latest known edition is given though some are no longer in print. — (Ed.)

What Is Discipleship?

Boreham, F. W., *Daily Readings*. Hodder & Stoughton 1976.
Miller, Keith and Larson, Bruce, *The Edge of Adventure: An Experiment in Faith*. Word 1974.
Morgan, G. Campbell, *Discipleship*. Allenson 1938.
*Weatherhead, Leslie D., *Discipleship*. SCM 1936.

God

Butterick, George A., *Prayer*. Abingdon Press 1982.
*Fosdick, Harry Emerson, *The Meaning of Prayer*. Abingdon Press Festival Ed. 1980.
Packer, James I., *Knowing God*. Hodder & Stoughton 1975.
Weatherhead, Leslie D., *Time for God*. Abingdon Press Festival Ed. 1981.
_____, *The Transforming Friendship*. Abingdon Press Festival Ed. 1977.

The Life of Jesus

Barclay, William, *Jesus as They Saw Him*. SCM 1977.
*Chesterton, G. K., *The Everlasting Man.* Burns & Oates 1974.
Cornell, George, *Behold the Man*. Word 1976.
Denney, James, *The Death of Christ.* Keats Publishing, USA 1981.

*Fosdick, Harry Emerson, *The Man from Nazareth*. Greenwood Press USA, 1978.

Glover, T. R., *The Jesus of History*. SCM 1928.

Guinness, H., *The Crux of Christianity*. Inter-Varsity Press 1963.

Guthrie, Donald, *Jesus the Messiah*. Pickering & Inglis 1972.

Morris, Leon, *Glory in the Cross*. Hodder & Stoughton 1966.

Morrison, Frank, *Who Moved the Stone?* Faber 1944.

Robertson, A. T., *Epochs in the Life of Christ*. Broadman Press USA.

Smyth, J. Paterson, *People's Life of Christ*. Hodder & Stoughton.

*Stalker, James R., *The Life of Jesus Christ*. T & T Clark 1928.

Stalker, James R., *The Trial & Death of Jesus Christ*. Hodder & Stoughton 1928.

*Stewart, James S., *The Life and Teaching of Jesus Christ*. St Andrew's Press 1977.

Weatherhead, Leslie D., *The Autobiography of Jesus*. Abingdon Press Festival Ed. 1980.

————, *The Meaning of the Cross*. Abingdon Press Festival Ed. 1982.

God's Moral Law

*Jones, E. Stanley, *The Christ of the Mount*. Abingdon Press 1985.

Spurgeon, C. H., *The Beatitudes*. Pilgrim Publications, USA 1978.

*Wesley, John, *Forty-four Sermons*. Epworth Press 1944. See especially sermons 16-28 on the Sermon on the Mount. (In the newest edition of these sermons, John Wesley's Fifty-three Sermons (Abingdon Press 1983), the sermons are numbers 12, 14, 15, 16, 18, 19, 20, 21, 22, 23 and 49.—Ed.)

The Character of Jesus

*Fosdick, Harry Emerson, *Twelve Tests of Character*. SCM 1924.

Jones, E. Stanley, *Victory Through Surrender*. Abingdon Press Festival Ed. 1980.

Murray, Andrew, *Absolute Surrender*. Marshall Morgan & Scott 1974.

*Weatherhead, Leslie D., *The Transforming Friendship*. Epworth Press 1956.

See also the books under The Life of Jesus.

The Kingdom of God — The Kingdom of Heaven

Jones, E. Stanley, *The Divine Yes*. Abingdon Press 1975.

Miller, Keith, and Larson, Bruce, *Living the Adventure: Faith and Hidden Difficulties*, Word 1976.

―――― , *The Passionate People*. Word. 1976.

Packer, James L., *I Want to Be a Christian*. Kingsway Publications 1977.

Routley, Erik, *Conversion*. Fortress Press 1978.

God is Love

*Drummond, Henry, *The Greatest Thing in the World*. Hodder & Stoughton 1980.

Lewis, C. S., *The Four Loves*. Fontana 1963.

Ogilvie, Lloyd J., *When God First Thought of You*. Word 1978.

*Tolstoy, Leo, Twenty-Three Tales. In *Great Short Works of Leo Tolstoy*. Harper & Row.

Whiston, Lionel, *For Those in Love*. Abingdon Press 1981.

The Life of Paul—The Book of Acts

Barclay, William, *Ambassador for Christ — The Life and Teaching of St Paul*. St Andrew's Press 1978.

Goodspeed, Edgar J., *Paul*. Abingdon Press 1981.

Pollock, John, *The Apostle*. Lion Publishing 1981.

* Stalker, James, *The Life of St Paul*. T & T Clark 1928.

The Epistle to the Romans—Paul's Gospel

Fisher, Wallace E., *All the Good Gifts: On Doing Bible Stewardship*. Augsburg, USA 1979.

* Fosdick, Harry Emerson, *The Meaning of Faith*. Abingdon Press 1982.

Palmer, Earl, *Salvation by Surprise: Studies in the Book of Romans*. Word 1975.

Yoder, Robert A., *Seeking First the Kingdom*. Herald Press, USA 1983.

The Holy Spirit

* Jones, E. Stanley, *The Christ of Every Road*. Abingdon Press 1930.

Lockyer, Herbert, *The Holy Spirit of God*. Abingdon Press 1983.

Morgan, G. Campbell, *The Spirit of God*. H. E. Walter 1972.

Ogilvie, Lloyd J., *You've Got Charisma*. Abingdon Press 1975.

Packer, James I., *Keep in Step with the Spirit*. Inter-Varsity Press 1984.

Victory

Bonhoeffer, Dietrich, *The Cost of Discipleship*. SCM Press 1964.

* Jones, E. Stanley, *Victorious Living*. Abingdon Press 1972.

* Reid, James, *The Victory of God*. Hodder & Stoughton 1928.

Bonhoeffer, Dietrich, *Life Together*. SCM Press 1954.

*Boreham, F. W., *A Bunch of Everlastings*. Epworth Press 1940.

Fosdick, Harry Emerson, *The Meaning of Service*. Abingdon Press Festival Ed. 1983.

Gustafson, Gus, *'I Was Called . . . To Be a Layman.'* Abingdon Press 1982.

Harris, Irving, *He Touched Me: Conversion Stories of Norman Vincent Peale, Bruce Larson, Ernest Gordon, Bill Wilson and Others*. Abingdon Press 1985.

Lovelace, Richard, *Dynamics of Spiritual Life*. Paternoster Press 1979.

Mohney, Nell, *The Inside Story: Personal Experiences of Faith*. The Upper Room 1979.

Baptism

Beasley-Murray, G. R., *Baptism in the New Testament*. Paternoster Press 1979.

Marty, Martin E., *Baptism*. Fortress Press 1977.

Murray, John, *Christian Baptism*. Baker Book House USA.

Willimon, William H., *Remember Who You Are: Baptism — A Model for Your Life*. The Upper Room 1980.

The Communion of the Lord's Supper

Marshall, I. Howard, *Last Supper and Lord's Supper*. Paternoster Press 1981.

Marty, Martin E., *The Lord's Supper*. Fortress Press 1980.

Ogilvie, Lloyd J., *Cup of Wonder*. Tyndale Press, USA 1976.

Willimon, William H., *Sunday Dinner*. The Upper Room 1981.

Biographies of Eric Liddell

Magnusson, Sally, *The Flying Scotsman*. Quartet Books 1981.

Thompson, D. P., *Eric H. Liddell, Athlete and Missionary*. Barnoak, Crieff, The Research Unit 1971. (now out of print)

Other Books Mentioned

Craig, A. C., Milligan, O. B., and Baillie, D. M., *Christian Faith and Practice*. First published 1932 by the Church of Scotland Committee on the Religious Instruction of Youth. Certain material has been made use of in this book by permission of the Church of Scotland Department of Education.

Rogers, Mrs Guy (ed.), *Morning Prayers and Readings for School and Family*. SCM Press 1931. Material used by permission.